ENDORSE

'A no-nonsense must-read for men everywhere! Demonstrating a unique understanding of men and masculinity, *Rethinking Masculinity* is a compelling and thought-provoking book addressing the unique challenges affecting the men of our generation.'

— Geraint Jones, Veteran and Sunday Times bestseller

'This book breaks the old paradigms of what it means to be a man. It will change lives. Each chapter challenges old thought processes and forces us to audit our position. It is an essential read for any man; I wish I had read this twenty years ago.'

— Matt Bowring, Fitness expert and personal trainer to A-list actors

'Essential reading for men feeling lost or wanting to live with greater purpose. Men don't just need help, they need strategies, and that is where this book delivers. It is a brilliant and comprehensive look at where we have come and where we need to go; empowering on every page.'

— Christian O'Connell, Multi award winning radio show host

'*Rethinking Masculinity* is a guide for living. It should be studied by every father and read to every son. Do not be fooled by the title, this book is valuable for both men and women. Women will gain incredible insight needed to better understand, support and advise the men in their life.'

— Anthony C. Gruppo, Former international CEO, author and philanthropist

'Dan's writing is extremely powerful and thought-provoking. I learnt so much from what he had to say. This is a timely, important book. We are currently facing a crisis in men's mental health like we've never experienced before. I know that Dan's words will have a big impact on everyone who reads them.'

— Jonny Benjamin MBE, Author and Founder of youth mental health charity, Beyond

'Dan has tackled a topic that deep down we all know exists, but we prefer not to think about – until now. This engaging and 'real-world' take is packed with practical tools for our modern times, and there's not a woke-ism in sight! It's powerful stuff and I've bought my three grown-up sons a copy each. You should do the same.'

— Nigel Bottrell, Founder of Entrepreneurs Circle

'Rather than simply opposing or re-writing old-school masculinity, Dan has demanded that it mature, gain feelings, gain a voice, and develop three-dimensions. This book offers masculinity a road to redemption that is defined by its strengths as well as by its blind spots. It is an intelligent, highly accessible and well-written read.'

— Russell Rose, BodyMind Psychotherapist. UKCP

'As middle-aged men, we often find ourselves stuck in a world where the measurements of success are career achievements and societal status symbols. *Rethinking Masculinity* offers a different view of this world. It offers men answers to the questions they're afraid to ask. It's the most important book that all middle-aged men absolutely must read.'

— Ryan Jones MBE, Former international rugby player and British & Irish Lion

'The concepts Dan shares in *Rethinking Masculinity* formed the framework of our coaching and have also changed my life; this book will change yours. It explains why and how professionally successful men struggle and provides the tools to make the changes needed to lead a genuinely fulfilling and successful life.'

— Matt Jones, CEO, award winning entrepreneur and communication expert

'A brilliant book and a must for any man, or partner of a man who feels a void in their life but can't identify its source. *Rethinking Masculinity* will help you find, understand and heal that inner void; it will leave you feeling as if you've summited the highest mountain – yourself.'

— Dave Hattam, Co-host of Lads, Dads and A Couple of Beers podcast

'The role of being a man has changed rapidly and significantly. This is a timely, well-written and thought-provoking book discussing what's important for men to understand about themselves and the world we live in.'

— Daniel Priestly, CEO, Dent Global

RETHINKING MASCULINITY

A modern man's guide to succeeding in life

DAN STANLEY
BETTERMEN FOUNDER

Rethink

First published in Great Britain in 2022 by Rethink Press (www.rethinkpress.com)

Author photo © Bradley Lever of The Content Creators

To my wife Rachael, for standing by my side, for being strong when I had no strength left, and to my beautiful children, Sophia and Spencer, the catalyst for all that I am

CONTENTS

FOREWORD

It's been twenty-seven years since the rugby union turned professional. When I first started playing for Wales in the mid-eighties, rugby was all about the macho, physical 'never show you're hurt' mentality. You were meant to be tough and masculine – to just get up and get on with it. Coaching and leadership meant having a few beers and a sing-song after the match to create a culture of hard work and camaraderie. It worked back then, but with both masculinity and sport undergoing fundamental changes, what got rugby here won't get rugby there: to the next level of global success.

Just like life, the rules of the game have changed. Success isn't only on the pitch any longer; it's on and off the field of play, meaning player welfare is more important than ever. As I've developed as a leader, I've learned that the modern game is all about creating an environment where people can be their best selves. The same is true in every arena of life. As leaders and members of society, we now have to create a culture of belonging and safety.

When I first connected with Dan Stanley, I was in the middle of a professionally tough period. Despite my years of career success, I had doubts about the space I was in and my future direction was unclear. We got to talking about leadership, my time as a coach and his time in the military. We discussed culture, how we lead people and how we support an environment that can get the best out of people; one where we all succeed. It turned out we had a lot of common understandings of leadership and a shared desire to see our people thrive, not just survive.

I did some coaching sessions with Dan and he had a profound effect on the way I now think about my professional career and life as a whole. He's insightful and knowledgeable to learn from, no matter where you are in your stage of life. He has a huge heart and passion for wanting to help people – particularly men.

His coaching equipped me with useful tools and techniques which I use in combination with my own experience to create strong world-class leadership results. He helped me to remove doubt and refocus on myself and my purpose. My purpose is my family. They drive me to become more, personally and professionally. Now I am an authentic leader of myself and a cultural architect of my organisation; I see myself as people-centred and competition ready.

If there's one thing you need to know about Dan, it's that he exudes loyalty and integrity. He gets the job done. In his book, Dan is giving you the opportunity to be the best version of yourself. You'll learn to look at success holistically and find opportunities to live life in ways that work for you. Above all, this book teaches you to be loyal to your truth – if something isn't working for you, don't avoid what you're feeling or experiencing. Instead, have a bias towards action and leading change for yourself.

This book is filled with life-changing insights and tools. Approach it with open-mindedness and you'll learn to live a happier and healthier life; a life you enjoy with the people you love.

My parting words are these – go on, have a go. Just try it.

Philip Davies
World Rugby, Director of Rugby; former international rugby player and BetterMen client

INTRODUCTION

There's nothing new about men losing their way. The opening sentence of Dante's *Inferno*, itself a story about man's journey written in the fourteenth century, is, 'Midway upon the journey of our life, I found myself within a dark forest, for the straightforward pathway had been lost'.[1]

Fast forward 700 years and a shocking number of modern men find themselves lost within our twenty-first century world and twenty-first century masculinity. Via societal conditioning, we're taught to prove our worth through work, ignore our feelings and discount our intuition. We put our noses to the grindstone, drudge through middle age and waste our finite time, all in the hope of a relaxing retirement.

Though we may achieve high levels of professional success, personally, we're often feeling frustratingly disconnected and unfulfilled. Men everywhere have fallen into a trap of our own making. If this resonates with you, know that you're not alone. In my mid-thirties, I felt this way, too.

As an award-winning ex-Army commando, a national sporting champion and key stakeholder in a multi-million-pound business, I'd ticked a lot of boxes, but I didn't feel how I expected to feel. This was compounded by the challenges of first-time fatherhood; I was left unsure of myself and my life's direction. Partly fuelled by my midlife crisis, I decided to take time out from the noise of life.

In that space, I realised that many other 'successful on paper' men were actually feeling the way I was. This sparked fundamental questions for me – is how we're living our lives the right way to live? Is our view of masculinity serving its purpose? I came to a sobering conclusion: no.

The purpose of this book is to challenge the status quo of modern masculinity and provoke thoughts that will, in turn, lead to change. My mission is to bust through the flawed thinking that professional success equals happiness and empower men of our era to redefine the standards of what it means to be a successful man. My hope for men who read this is that they choose to create a more fulfilling and aligned life from the inside out.

This book is a call to arms for any man who has experienced a setback, finds himself stagnant in midlife or is silently enduring the second half of his life. It's a guide for any man who is questioning 'Is this it?' or fears his best years are behind him.

In the chapters ahead, I will use the term 'career' to describe both those men who are in the corporate space and those who are business owners and leaders. I'll use the term 'client' to describe those I've coached. Though 'client' may sound transactional, it's a relevant description of the men who choose to partner with me.

The journey ahead will question everything you may think you know, but don't be shut down by fear of change. Paraphrasing the words of personal development pioneer Leland Val Van de Wall, the degree to which a man can grow is directly proportionate to the amount of personal truth he can accept without shutting down or running away.

If you're ready to cultivate real change, live a better life, leave a better legacy for your sons and daughters and reshape masculinity itself, then this is the book for you. In the next nine chapters, I'll teach you how to stop trying to live up to societal success and instead live a life you're proud of. Your future is what you make it...

PART ONE

UNDERSTANDING MASCULINITY

1

Twenty-first Century Masculinity

I'll be honest: you probably won't want to hear what I'm about to share, but the fact that you picked up this book shows a part of you knows you need to hear it. The truth is, many men today are feeling lost. They are unknowingly living a default life, dictated by parental conditioning, societal norms and commercial consumerism. Time flashes by as they get caught up in living professionally successful but unfulfilling lives.

Modern men strive to achieve success. From the outside, it seems like their lives are 'textbook' perfect – they have the German car, the expensive house, the beautiful family, but underneath the surface, these men are struggling by the time they reach middle age and begin the second half of their lives. Their career is defined by firefighting. A full diary means no time to focus on family, health or friends (the things they say they value). Their relationship with their partner feels distant, as does their connection with their children. Health and fitness have taken a back seat for years.

When you see a man who's successful, you're seeing the result of his effort. You're not seeing what it's taken for him, and from him, to get where he is. The reality is, this default path takes a lot. In this situation, men feel like they have to hide their dissatisfaction, believing that they're alone in feeling this way. Part of the 'silent majority', they're quietly suffering and letting the days pass them by without truly understanding the consequences of their inaction.

I've been there, too. Having ticked many of the 'right' boxes, I was pretty secure in the fact that I was winning in the game of life, but deep down, I felt exactly like the men I described above. Then, I reached a breaking point as I became a father and began to assess my life. Unlike what many men experience, my break was a breakthrough and I wound up recalibrating my life. With a new focus on purpose, fulfilment and legacy, I have successfully left behind my superficially successful past.

Now I want to share my message and experience with other men who already suspect there's more to life than work, but find themselves asking, 'What template of life am I meant to follow?' Masculinity is at a crossroads and the men of our era get to choose which direction we lead ourselves and future generations of men; to craft our legacy. As ancient Greek politician Pericles said, 'What you leave behind is not what is engraved in stone monuments, but what is woven into the lives of others.'

I have moved away from what I call the old blueprint of masculinity, the default template. Instead, I propose the BetterMen blueprint, which encourages men to live an intentional life, defined by high levels of presence, purpose and performance – a life by design. Men following this blueprint develop clear life goals and purpose-driven habits.

My promise to you is that if you approach this book with an open mind, you will be rewarded with life-changing realisations and the skills for a happy and purposeful new life. As Chinese philosopher Confucius said, 'We have two lives; the second begins when we realise we only have one.' Consider this the beginning of your second life. In this chapter, you'll start to understand the common problems with masculinity as we experience it today, many of which may resonate with you.

THE OLD BLUEPRINT OF MASCULINITY

The path to a happier, healthier and more meaningful life as a high-performing man starts with understanding the root of the problem. From the moment we were born, we have been exposed to cultural expectations, media and social hierarchies that handed us a blueprint of masculinity we still unconsciously follow to this day. The problem? That blueprint, passed down from our fathers' and grandfathers' generation, is no longer fit for purpose in our digitally connected twenty-first-century world.

Let's dive into the roots of this blueprint.

Childhood conditioning

If you're old enough, cast your mind back to the popular TV shows and films on air in the seventies and eighties. Young boys everywhere watched in awe as Schwarzenegger, Stallone and Van Damme ran, punched and shot their way across the screen. Now think about the famous football and rugby players of the day. The strong, unemotional machines at peak physical performance. Think about the fathers on TV shows, acting as the fearsome disciplinarian. Across media and sports, young boys saw adult men as detached, physically strong and decisive.

These male archetypes bled from the screen and into real life on the playground at school. Boys were encouraged to play rough, join sports teams and excel physically, but the enjoyment of exercise was marred by a sense of needing to outperform peers and, for personal safety in the playground, adopt an attitude of conformity and 'survival of the strongest'. Many were told to be strong and to 'man up' because 'boys don't cry'. Perhaps their fathers also embodied these traits.

Young boys were taught to always exhibit 'appropriate' gender behaviours. If they didn't uphold those expectations, they were likely ridiculed and made to feel different, to feel inferior. This stopped them from expressing how they felt. Boys learned to suppress their feelings, reject their emotions and numb their experience. Every single day, they were conditioned to believe that this narrow, one-dimensional definition of masculinity was 'the' blueprint: a blueprint that they would have to follow to be successful and to be a 'real man' in adulthood.

Present-day masculinity

As they grew up, most boys of this generation followed the blueprint and are the middle-aged men of today, many of them on the upward curve in their careers. They got married, had 2.4 children and bought a dog. They see themselves as providers and breadwinners and they identify with the 'traditional' masculine traits of being strong, silent and successful.

In the 'game of life', these men may feel they're winning, but underneath that thin veneer of success... it seems more like they're losing. Countless men question, 'Is this it...?' and spend hours analysing, procrastinating and ruminating – stuck in their own head. Staring at the phone screen, they lose time on social media, scrolling through their feeds and seeing men with bigger houses, nicer cars and seemingly perfect relationships, because no one's posting the truth of their reality.

Many men actually feel alone, isolated and lost in their own thoughts. My clients have told me that they feel like they are physically in the room with their families, but not really present. They come home from work to their children talking about their day at school, but it all seems so trivial, my clients just can't engage. They can't switch off from work and connect.

The novelist Mark Twain once said, 'The worst loneliness is to not be comfortable with yourself.' Modern men are on an uncomfortable path of loneliness and real but confusing unhappiness. The problem is, we've been taught *what* to think, not *how* to think. In our modern world, the one-dimensional model of masculinity, of protecting and providing, isn't enough.

We'll now unpack some of the main challenges contributing to the sense of unhappiness and unease that so many men face, particularly in middle age. If you see yourself in these pages, know that you are not alone and that this book will provide answers, enabling you to live a more aligned and meaningful life.

CHALLENGE 1: WORKAHOLISM AND BURNOUT

Adhering to strict gender roles, countless men (including me) got jobs and started climbing the career ladder from an early age. What nobody told us is that the ladder can quickly become a slippery slope, leading to workaholism, and then burnout.

The addiction of workaholism

Workaholism starts with us enthusiastically contributing to a career or business, but over time transforms into us developing obsessive perfectionist traits. The weight of work becomes a looming shadow over everything. Late nights in the office are fuelled by high levels of stress and this becomes the norm. Family members and friends recognise that the workaholic is spending less time with them; the workaholic feels a sense of guilt for choosing work over life, but they do it anyway.

Being addicted to work is a genuine problem, but it has somehow become accepted by society and accepted in marriages as a valid reason not to put the time and effort in. As we'll discuss later, it's also a contributing factor in divorce. Many men don't even know that they may be workaholics.

Some key warning signs are:

- Thinking of how to free up more time to work
- Spending much more time working than originally planned
- Working to reduce feelings of guilt or anxiety
- Becoming stressed if prohibited from working
- Deprioritising hobbies, leisure activities and exercise because of work

This likely resonates for a lot of high-performing men. Work completely takes over their lives. Have you ever stopped to consider why it is that when you ask someone what they do, their immediate response is usually their job title? This is the societal conditioning I'll be sharing more about later.

With the increase in working from home, the line between work and life has blurred even further. Losing the commute means that many professional men are now unable to switch off in their own home. While they're on important calls, loved ones expect them to be available because they're in the home. My clients describe tip-toeing into the kitchen to boil the kettle, hoping not to have their work interrupted by the trivialities of family life. The delicate knife-edge that so many men were balancing on before the COVID-19 pandemic has been tipped. Burnout is more common than ever – a survey of 2,000 British workers highlighted this, as over 73% of respondents stated that they felt burned out after the pandemic.[1]

The five stages of burnout

It's possible you already know what burnout feels like, either from personal experience or having witnessed the implosion of a colleague or peer. For confirmation, it feels like a constant state of exhaustion, anxiousness, isolation and irritability. It feels like waking up in the morning after a terrible night's sleep with a sense of dread, while pretending that everything is 'OK'. Knowing that you'll be constantly firefighting. Not being able to take a lunch break. Coming home and collapsing on the sofa, feeling apathetic and bingeing on Netflix and social media because, sadly, that's the only thing you can muster the energy to do.

How does being the 'classic workaholic' get to this point? There are five defined stages that may lead to burnout.[2]

The first stage is the **honeymoon phase**. This simply involves high job satisfaction and is a normal and healthy beginning to any role. Next, the **stress** begins. Work becomes harder and less enjoyable, optimism may fade and feelings of stress creep in. This may manifest as a lack of sleep, headaches and no social interaction.

Stage three is **chronic stress**, in which high levels of stress are felt frequently. This, of course, leads to **burnout**, when symptoms of stress become critical. It's impossible to continue as normal and it's increasingly difficult to cope. People with burnout feel helpless, trapped, unmotivated and detached. Finally, **habitual burnout** means that these symptoms have become ingrained in day-to-day life, creating ongoing mental, physical and emotional challenges.

Believe me, men all over the country are experiencing this. Perhaps you're feeling burned out, too. If you are, using the scale above, what stage are you at? Burnout is all too common, and with it, other challenges arise.

Let's explore another challenge delivered by the old blueprint of masculinity: loneliness.

CHALLENGE 2: LONELINESS

Shortly before I started to write this book, I was out for a run while listening to a podcast. The host asked, 'In your hour of need, who would you call?' This sparked an uncomfortable moment of self-reflection for me.

I realised that I would not call my childhood best friends, the men who had been best men at my wedding. We were on completely different life trajectories. For years, we'd been going through the motions, saying we'd meet up but 'life' would always get in the way. In reality, we were just in different places. This made me angry at first. Then it made me think.

Many male friendships are based on past experiences, like playing sports or going to school or university together. They're transient, based on a moment in time. This is probably why we drift, leading to 32% of men stating they don't have a best friend.[3] Reports show, in fact, that 35% of men admit to feeling lonely at least once a week and that 10% would prefer to keep this hidden because of internal shame.[4] Because men's feelings are underreported, it's likely that these numbers are, in reality, much higher than this.

When you take into consideration the extraordinary numbers of men experiencing workaholism and burnout, it's no surprise that there is an epidemic of real and deep male loneliness. Socrates, a Greek philosopher considered a forefather of Stoicism, said, 'Beware the barrenness of a busy life.' There is a lot of wisdom in those words. Men find themselves so busy that life becomes empty, but there's more to this puzzle and a key piece is not discussing our feelings.

Resistance to discussing feelings

Men's loneliness is compounded by a resistance to speaking about and discussing their feelings. In fact, 38% of men say that they have avoided talking to others about how they feel so as not to appear unmanly,[5] but isolation leads to amplification of problems. Many men (43%) wish that they could talk more to others about personal problems they have experienced.[6] There is an incorrect but shame-inducing sense that talking about their feelings makes them 'weak'. This leaves a lot of men feeling trapped, unable to speak up.

One participant in a Movember UK survey of men aged forty-five to fifty-four stated, 'To be manly is to always try to act tough even when you feel like you just want to break down and cry.'[7] All too often, men 'armour up' to protect themselves from the perceived judgement of others, but never thinking about, expressing or discussing our feelings results in a deep loneliness.

I often hear my clients say things like, 'I don't believe I am allowed to feel like I am struggling, but I am'; 'I mean, I should be grateful for what I've achieved, but I am not'; 'Compared to what's happening in the world, my problems aren't that bad'. As we will discuss, lots of men feel this way, but because we learn by modelling other men, we have no idea we aren't alone.

The impact of social media

Convenient but superficial digital connections only make things worse. We are lonelier than ever, watching our network's lives unfold through a little screen in our hands, instead of experiencing their lives with them. COVID-19 has only made this worse, with screen time increasing by 50–70% during the pandemic.[8]

To be clear, I am not against social media; it has given a powerful and necessary voice to prominent social issues. What I am against is how we as a society exploit the ease and expedient nature of our digitally connected 'togetherness'.

Even before the prominence of Facebook, Instagram and LinkedIn, men were skilled at keeping conversations at a surface and superficial level. Now, interacting through a device, face conveniently hidden from view, many men have mastered the art of avoiding and evading any conversation that might require them to reveal how they feel. Their screens become a mask for their loneliness.

The risks of loneliness

Being lonely is a risk. Social relationships have been proven to protect both mental and physical wellbeing. As demonstrated in the seventy-five-year longitudinal Harvard Happiness Study, people with meaningful social relationships are happier, have better long-term health and live longer than those without.[9] From decreasing stress and heart disease to increasing resilience, friendships do a lot more than we may think.

Isolation, on the other hand, only makes things worse. Problems become bigger in the vacuum of one's own mind. Clearly, something in the blueprint of what it means to be a man isn't working anymore. Men are left isolated, overworked and lonely.

This leads us to our next challenge: ongoing poor mental health.

CHALLENGE 3: POOR MENTAL HEALTH

There is a crisis in men's mental health today. A report by BeyondBlue support service says, 'On average, one in eight men will experience depression and one in five will experience anxiety in the course of their lives'.[10] Actually, we can deduce that it's probably much more than that as men feel pressured and unable to discuss their feelings or mental health. This means that a large number of men's mental-health issues sadly go unreported.

Depression, anxiety and loneliness

Depression can be described as a low mood, a lack of interest in enjoyable activities and, at the extreme, suicidal thoughts. It's a harbouring of sadness. Anxiety, on the other hand, is excessive worry and restlessness. It's a fear of the future, a life yet to be lived.

Many men feel overwhelmed in their work and unable to safely communicate their emotional needs, meaning we see sobering statistics on men's mental health, such as the fact that men aged forty to forty-nine have the highest suicide rates in the UK.[11] Men are also less likely to access psychological therapies than women: in the UK, only 36% of referrals to National Health Service talking therapies are for men.[12]

A common cause of poor mental health

The truth is, an overwhelming number of professionally successful men feel mentally busy, emotionally numb and physically tired. They hide from their feeling of discomfort and their sense that something is amiss by working more. As a result, they have no free time to spend on themselves or with the people they love. Over time, they can develop anxiety and depression, but stay silent because of the stigma and shame that is still attached to poor mental health.

A key element of this problem is the fact that men have been working to achieve the goals of others, chasing and trying to live up to societal success instead of living a life they enjoy. They've been ticking boxes in the 'game of life' with a rat-race mentality, not just keeping up with the Joneses, but beating them; constantly upgrading their house, car and holidays, without stopping to think if any of it really makes them happy. Their self-esteem is tied to their possessions, their diary reflects their priorities and their priorities are unquestionably work related. There is no room for real connection with others or themselves.

Lowering the numbers of male suicide and improving men's mental health means enabling men to seek support and ask for help. Personal happiness is available to every man, but it has to be consciously chosen. Contrary to previous eras, we as men are now proving that we can't win at the game of life without high levels of real happiness.

CHALLENGE 4: MIDLIFE CRISIS

A midlife crisis is a well-known cultural phenomenon. It's usually sparked in middle age, which is a period in a man's life where he tends to question who he is, where he's going and who he's going with. During this time, many men will also question the validity of what they have achieved in life so far and worry about what's next for them. When this happens, men can feel lost, isolated and disconnected. It becomes a crisis.

Swiss explorer Bertrand Piccard said, 'A crisis accepted becomes an adventure and an adventure that we refuse will remain a crisis.' Unfortunately, the vast majority of middle-aged men end up with a crisis. They fall back on stereotypical releases, like buying a new car, learning to ride a motorbike, having a flirt or a fling, buying a new watch or signing up to some sort of physical challenge. Unsurprisingly, none of these things actually work; they just suppress, mask or delay the inevitability of the real issue.

The roots of a midlife crisis

There is often a gap between who we are and who we pretend to be. The bigger the gap, the bigger the void in our life and the greater our susceptibility to a midlife crisis. We may own the societal symbols of success and have the picture-perfect social-media profile, but if what we have isn't what we need, more of the same won't help.

We can have everything a man could need by the standards of societal success, but if these standards are wrong or outdated, then we'll never experience life as we expect it. That's exactly why we need to rethink and redefine the standards of modern-day masculinity.

It's hard to break ingrained habits and redefine standards. Many of my clients feel there's a sunk cost in their current way of living and they don't have the capacity to start again as they've invested so much into it. They find themselves struggling (which leads to more struggle). It's a crisis.

CHALLENGE 5: DIVORCE

A key indicator of successful masculinity in the traditional blueprint is getting married, but the problem is, expectations of what a marriage is have shifted. Men used to be the breadwinners and women were expected to stay home and look after the children. That's far from the case now. Societally, things are shifting, but often this hasn't yet caught up within the household, causing discord.

Men still feel they need to be the providers, which means workaholism leads to them taking their loved ones for granted. I find the old adage 'work gets the best of me, life gets what's left of me' fitting here to describe the situation. With no time invested in their relationship, couples lose the currency of intimacy: appreciation. Small frustrations snowball to resentments, and with men feeling unable to talk about their feelings, this then leads to distance. On top of all this, a sense of 'keeping up appearances' adds pressure to make it seem that all is well when actually, it's falling apart.

Many of my clients, when they eventually slow down and look up, find themselves in a marriage of practicality. They've become so busy working, looking after the house and raising the children that their marital drift has become tangible; there's no real relationship, connection or depth. They may be lying inches apart from their partner in bed every night, but they're miles apart in terms of connection.

Nobody wants to be in that situation, but after some time it becomes unmanageable and the only solution seems like divorce. The UK divorce rate is estimated at 42%, and in fact, over 100,000 British couples got a divorce in 2019. The average male divorce age is forty-six to forty-nine.[13]

The COVID pandemic pulled back the curtain on what is happening behind closed doors: people just aren't happy in their relationships. In 2020, the first year of the pandemic, divorce enquiries rose by a significant 122%.[14] Social media impacts this, too, as 'perfect relationships' are projected online with no insight into what's really happening. The distance between people seems to keep on growing.

YOU'RE NOT ALONE

That's a brief introduction to the five key challenges of masculinity in the twenty-first century. Do you know what binds them all together? A feeling of shame. A feeling of being unable to talk about what life actually feels like. A feeling of isolation, inadequacy and loneliness. This is exactly the reason why these problems persist: because as men, we're not talking about them, we're not owning them and we're falling into traps of our own making.

I have little respect for the old blueprint of masculinity, the one that has caused the challenges I've shared. The system is no longer fit for purpose. When we're boys, the old blueprint tells us there are three things that we need to be a man:

- We have to be strong. It's the old, unhelpful narrative that big boys don't cry.

- We should be silent. It's much like the first rule of fight club – the first rule of being a man is don't talk about what it's like to be a man.

- Despite the now obvious costs to health and happiness, we have to be professionally successful.

This trifecta of intergenerational toxicity and conditioning is responsible for causing many of the problems modern men are experiencing.

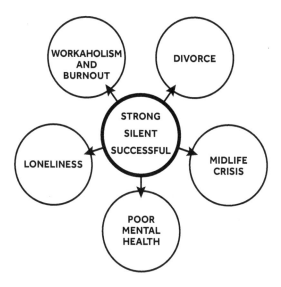

The five challenges facing modern-day masculinity

I know as a gender, we can do and become better. I want men who are facing any of the five challenges above to know that they are not alone. I want them to start talking about it and taking proactive measures, like those you'll find in this book, to realign their lives and craft legacies they'll be proud of.

My client work and the men's walking group I lead, Men & Mountains, have shown me that men don't actually need much prompting to talk about these challenges. It's natural to talk. When we take away the artificial structure around what men can and can't say 'because they're men', we reach an understanding and can talk freely.

Peer-to-peer sharing is important because when there's commonality of experience and reasoning, it creates a high degree of psychological and emotional safely. This makes sharing our authentic selves more permissible and encourages us to be more expressive: a key factor in promoting positive personal wellbeing. Essentially, when we as men have psychological safety, it's as if everything is able to come up and out.

Understanding this is the first step to throwing off the shackles of the old blueprint. We can take control. We're responsible for what we do and don't do; our decisions shape our direction. A few key mindset and lifestyle shifts can cause significant ripple effects that change our life's trajectory, something my clients have experienced time and time again.

My clients are the men who do the work to live with greater life clarity and deliberate purpose. They become effective leaders of themselves. They are living and role modelling a better version of masculinity and passing on a meaningful, lasting legacy. Are you ready to join them?

With this book, I aim to help you bust through the myth of masculinity, the flawed thinking that professional success equals personal happiness. It hasn't in the past; it doesn't. It won't. It's time to forget manning up and instead open up, because everything we as men do now matters. Society is at a crossroads when it comes to masculinity – and we decide our direction.

We'll talk more about fear later on in the book, but at this stage, I'll simply share with you the words of George Adair, a real-estate developer in the USA in the years following the Civil War: 'Everything you've ever wanted is on the other side of fear.' Don't allow yourself to be shut down, turn away from or ignore the discomfort of your day-to-day life. A man's work starts in pain. The pain you feel in your life, the frustration and dissatisfaction, is a message. Listen to it and learn from it as it's a message from yourself – your true self. After all the hard yards to get to where you are, you deserve to live a happy, healthy, fulfilling and successful life. Let's make it happen and step into the next chapter.

REFLECTION EXERCISES

Tony Robbins, the world-renowned personal-development 'guru', stated that, 'The quality of your life is a direct reflection of the quality of the questions you are asking yourself'.[15] This is exactly why we'll be working on a reflection section at the end of every chapter.

It's important to approach these sections with an open mind and, if it's your thing, a pen and paper. This enables you to actively complete the exercises as you navigate through the book. Via thought-provoking questions, directly related to the chapter you've just read, these reflection sections will raise your levels of awareness and, if you commit to it, lay the foundations of meaningful change. If you feel like these questions detract from your read flow, feel free to read the book in its entirety, and then circle back to each of the nine reflection sections.

- If you were to honestly describe your current experience of life in only three words, what would those words be? Write them down somewhere safe or store them in your phone; you'll need them at the end of the book.

- Considering your life at your age and stage, are you where you thought you wanted to be? If not, why not?

- Regardless of your current mental-health state, what could you do more and less of to improve it?

- Like the question that stopped me in my tracks: who would you call in your hour of need and why?

- If someone you cared about was experiencing a midlife crisis, what advice would you give them?

- If you're in a relationship or marriage, on a scale of one to ten, one being low, ten being high, what score would you give it and why?

2

The History Of
Modern-day Masculinity

The time has come to stop ignoring the issues that are affecting masculinity today. We men who have been adversely impacted by the old blueprint have to start talking about the fact that it's simply no longer serving us. Workaholism, loneliness, poor mental health, midlife crisis and divorce – this is not the experience we were put on Earth to have. I'm guessing you know this, deep within yourself. It's likely why you picked up this book.

We, the men of our era, have the responsibility to craft a new blueprint of masculinity that enables a life-fulfilling 'masculine success'. Something better and more natural, not guided by socially imposed boundaries or gender stereotypes. We deserve this, and so do our sons and future generations of boys and men.

Think about the kind of legacy we're leaving them now. They're learning that men stay locked away in their offices all day, and locked away in their own heads, too. We're teaching them that to be happy, they need money, that they need holidays to take breaks from their lives, and that friendships are low-priority and digital.

How do we go about crafting a legacy of a healthy, purpose-driven blueprint? We'll first need to look into the legacy we were left with. In this chapter, we'll dive into the history of 'what it means to be a man' and really examine the gender roles we've been conditioned to adhere to. Then, we'll look at present-day society and consider how our ideas about masculinity need to evolve. We have the opportunity to reshape the meaning of being a 'man' and the legacy we are leaving behind, and that starts here and now with you and me.

GENDER ROLES SINCE THE INDUSTRIAL REVOLUTION

During the eighteenth century, society fundamentally shifted with the dawn of the Industrial Revolution. The worlds of work and family life transformed in a way that catalysed and cemented the strict gender roles you and I have been following most of our lives.[1]

Before the Industrial Revolution, the predominance of agrarian farming culture meant that the household was the centre of production. Married couples and their children would work together in the fields of their farm, or in their homes, crafting textiles and cloth, which they'd sell. While gender roles certainly existed, the responsibility of providing for the family fell on both the man and the woman.

Then, with the advent of the Industrial Revolution, men began working outside of the home in factories. They sold their time to factory owners, who used that time to make mass-produced goods. Some men even moved away from their homes to the cities so that they could provide for their families. Women stayed home alone, tending to their children and running the household. Their inherent purpose shifted to giving birth and raising children. The days of working alongside their husbands on the farm were long gone.

Men, on the other hand, didn't have a given birth purpose, and so they sought that purpose in work. Gender roles became distinct and clearly defined: Mum nurtures; Dad works, and what difficult work it was, too. Factory jobs were gruelling and dangerous. Men would come home exhausted with no mental capacity to tend to the emotional needs of themselves or their families – something that might ring true with men of today. Many were engaged in backbreaking labour, but all that mattered was that they made money. They were the sole breadwinners for their families. Over time, the amount of money a man brought home became the measure of his worth.

Some of this sounds familiar, doesn't it? Growing up, you likely learned that this is just the way things are. Men are the breadwinners. The problem is, those gender roles may have lifted us into the modern age, supporting the innovation of the Industrial Revolution, but things have significantly changed since then. Back in the 1800s, life expectancy hovered around thirty to forty years – we're now collectively living to be well over eighty. What are we using that extra time for? Most likely, more work. There are no guidelines, so many men live through these extra years lacking purpose. With blinkers on, they get on the work treadmill until it's time to retire.

The effects of the world wars

History in many ways continues to build and impact the society we live in today. After the Industrial Revolution came war. The two world wars of the twentieth century were the largest military conflicts in recorded history; 8.5 million men died in battle in the First World War, 15 million in the Second World War.[2][3] These conflicts fundamentally changed the bodies and minds of generations of men. The ones who made it home came back severely traumatised, but the trauma of their experience went unrecognised and was largely swept under the rug of the British societal 'stiff upper lip' and 'keep calm and carry on' rhetoric.

The prevailing post-war narrative showed heroes coming home and building a better, healthier, more peaceful society. They got married, bought houses and had children (resulting in the 'baby boom' after the Second World War). The unspoken truth that hospitals were filled with veterans, dads, suffering from serious mental-health problems was ignored. Shell shock was the only phrase these veterans had to describe symptoms that left them feeling helpless as they were affected by panic, fear and an inability to sleep, reason or talk. Nowadays, shell shock is more accurately called post-traumatic stress disorder (PTSD) and patients receive excellent care from a range of organisations.

Fatherhood post-war

Fatherhood is hard enough as it is. Young boys look up to their fathers to learn and understand moral virtues, rites of passage and how to interact with the world. When you add the severe trauma and poor mental health caused by experiencing the horrors of war, it makes father-son dynamics even more complex.

That's what the post-war generation of men experienced. With no diagnosis for PTSD (the disorder was only officially recognised in 1980),[4] many post-war fathers were unhappy and mentally unwell, but unable to discuss or process what they had been through. They were expected to carry on as normal and function as providers and heads of the household, but wartime dads were damaged dads, unable to equate the horrors they'd seen in war with their domestic lives back home.

As a result, many young boys were raised by fathers who were emotionally distant, irritable and prone to unexpected outbursts. Often veterans of World War Two had trouble sleeping and turned to alcohol for support, or were distracted or unavailable. Young boys learned that men simply didn't talk about their emotions. Empathy, compassion and emotional literacy fell to the bottom of the barrel when boys were being taught what it means to be a man.

These children, with distant and unemotional fathers, grew up and went on to raise the middle-aged men of today. Those traits have been passed on through two generations. History is a lot closer than it seems.

Fatherhood through recent history

A father's physical absence is just as impactful on a young boy as emotional absence. In recent history, the UK has been increasingly facing a crisis of absent fatherhood.

There are now 236 areas across England and Wales where at least 50% of households have no dad present.[5] This lack of male role modelling is also seen in the education system, as teaching was previously regarded as a 'womanly' pursuit, discouraging men from becoming teachers. One in four primary schools has no male teacher and 80% have fewer than three.[6]

What does that mean for fatherless boys? The stats show that it makes for a much harder life: 71% of those who don't complete secondary school are fatherless.[7] One study tells us, 'Similarly, father absence can increase the risk of using illicit substances at a younger age.'[8]

It's a vicious cycle, with boys growing up to be emotionally absent men, feeling distant in their own relationships, and then burning out, leaving home or getting divorces. Due to split custody, they are often unable to spend as much time as they'd like with their child, perpetuating the cycle of boys without engaged fathers.

To summarise, many men have grown up looking for a blueprint of masculinity elsewhere, due to having had an emotionally or, equally important, physically absent father. With no role model for 'what it means to be a man' in childhood, these men feel disconnected from their emotions and themselves as adults. They misinterpret Stoicism as emotionlessness and confuse resilience with the belief that quitters never win and winners never quit. They have been taught the skill of self-repression instead of self-expression, leading to a crisis of masculinity today.

The present day

In a world low on 'healthy' male role models, men have turned to the unemotional 'alpha male' blueprint that may have worked once, but no longer applies to our changing world. Many men find themselves holding on to outdated traditional values at the risk of falling on their swords, and I can see why. Losing a clear image of who you will be in the future can be disconcerting. It can leave a man who's wanting to change feeling adrift, unsure and anxious of who he should be now.

It's time to face reality – everything from gender roles to work culture and lifestyle choices have been thrown up into the air by changing norms.

GENDER ROLES TODAY

It's no longer solely a man's world. Everything is changing, but where does that leave the men who follow the old blueprint? They're now lacking purpose and direction, unsure of themselves, their future and their legacy.

Work

There has been a recent shift towards diversity and inclusion, focusing on equality for women in the workplace. Women are taking on traditionally masculine traits to achieve high levels of success and personal independence, while bringing more uniquely feminine traits to the table. This is, to be clear, a much-needed movement, but the issue is, women in the workforce describe feeling the need to act more 'masculine' to succeed. Everyone is structuring their behaviour towards this outdated, one-dimensional blueprint of leadership because that has been seen as the path to success.

High-performing men in this shifting work landscape find themselves unsure of how to act or behave. With no legacy of positive purpose-driven male leadership to follow, they are in new territory.

Earlier generations of men had jobs, not careers. They didn't have mobiles, emails or WhatsApp; their job was simply a job for life. Now, men are part of complex working cultures in which emotional intelligence is rewarded as much as the hard graft. Furthermore, high-performing men feel like they're spread more thinly than ever – and the truth is, they are. They're trying to prove their worth through work while balancing a healthy home life.

What can we do to feel comfortable within this system? As women don't need to become more masculine, we as men don't need to become more feminine – we simply all need to be more human. We need to have greater awareness, be more open and bring our authentic selves to the world. This is our first step to feeling more comfortable outside of the old blueprint.

A new type of masculine leadership is needed now, one that encapsulates the soft skills, too. The problem with the old method of leadership has become clear: if all we have in our leadership tool box is a hammer, every problem we see is a nail.

Relationships

Women now earn more than their male partners in almost 25% of UK households, up from 19% in 2004.[9] This shift is only increasing, as the number of female directors in FTSE 100 companies has risen by 50% in five years.[10] While this may not be true in your household, it reflects changing attitudes towards the split of gender roles and responsibilities in heterosexual relationships: sharing financial responsibility and childcare is becoming normal and perhaps expected. Just like the old blueprint of masculinity, traditional gender roles are simply no longer fit for purpose as they do not reflect the reality of life for many couples today.

This is exactly why the old blueprint doesn't work when it's applied to marriages today. It was based on gender roles and ideas about husbands and wives that have changed and moved on. For example, you may have heard the adage that a happy wife = happy life, no questions asked. This concept is based on old ideas of creating superficial surface happiness. I wonder how many men try to make their partner happy at their own expense because of this.

Think about the stereotypical way we as men have been taught to 'act' in a relationship. If our partner is angry? Bring home some supermarket or garage flowers. Are they moaning about something? Do one of the household chores we've been putting off, because that's easier than opening up and asking what's wrong. Moving beyond the unemotional too-tired-to-talk stereotype of a husband we may have seen on TV or perhaps from our own father is key. If only one half of a relationship is happy, it simply won't function, let alone flourish.

In the old blueprint we were handed down, nobody taught us how to openly express ourselves to our partner. Sure, we may think we're expressing our affection and feelings, but do we truly understand how they like to receive our love? Love is a language and if we're speaking a language our partner doesn't understand, we're setting ourselves up to fail.

The five love languages, developed by author and counsellor Gary Chapman,[11] are a useful way to look at how you express your feelings to your partner. Think about yourself and your partner. Which of these languages do you relate to the most?

The first love language is **words of affirmation**. People using words of affirmation appreciate verbal acknowledgements of affection. This means frequent 'I love yous' and encouragement. The next is **quality time.** These people appreciate, above all else, time spent together, including active listening, eye contact and full presence. The third is **acts of service**, where someone goes out of their way to lighten the load of their partner. This could be anything from bringing them coffee to doing their laundry. The fourth is **gifts**: a partner going out of their way to arrange a visual token of their love. Finally, the fifth love language is **physical touch**. These people feel most appreciated with frequent physical signs of affection.

Men are taught through TV shows, films and targeted advertising that acts of service and gifts are the two most important love languages, but the truth is, those are weak foundations for marital success. Having emotional intimacy is what connects couples – being open, actively engaged and supportive. It's no wonder that divorce rates are higher than ever; we've simply been taught the wrong things about love and relationships.

MASCULINITY IN A CHAOTIC WORLD

Countries around the world are polarised on almost every major issue. There's an all-or-nothing attitude and a growing sense that we're all playing in a zero sum game.

Within this chaos, our sense of self can easily become lost in 'things'. Seemingly, as a society, we're yet to learn that consumerism won't fill the void between our professional success and personal dissatisfaction. We can't buy our way out of unhappiness, but we've been led to believe we can so we try anyway. We know that material things bring nothing more than fleeting happiness, but if we're stuck on the hamster wheel, we still invest thousands of pounds in these items.

As journalist Matt Rudd states, 'The system set up by men for men is failing us'. Many men lead themselves and their families into this system, frantically spending and consuming, which keeps them trapped in a job they hate as they need to keep feeding the machine. What kind of men are we in this system? Think about this: even if we're winning the rat race, at the end of the day, we're still a rat.

Teaching yourself to step away from this and inviting yourself to rethink masculinity, to recalibrate your life and lead yourself with intent, is key to a healthy and happy future for everyone. Now more than ever, an updated purpose-driven view of masculinity is needed. Knowing who you are and what you stand for is vital for moving from a confusing and chaotic life to a contented and compelling one.

Your legacy is our legacy

With this complicated history and even more difficult present day, many men are currently trying to excel in a life they don't understand. We need to think collectively as a gender – what are the men of our era leaving behind? Our sons are tomorrow's men. They matter and we have a responsibility not to pass on the baggage we've inherited: the same baggage that's creating such disturbing figures around mental health, burnout, divorce and loneliness.

If you're a father, think about how your children are being or have been raised. Are they watching you escape the stress of day-to-day life through package holidays, grabbing takeaways because food needs to be fast and convenient, FaceTiming Granny and Grandad because digital connections are more efficient and ignoring exercise because health is something only people with time do? What kind of role model is that for your sons and daughters to look up to while they're developing their own values and sense of purpose?

Our purpose is not dictated by the men who have come before us. Our family role is not solely to provide and protect. It's not too late. Our individual and collective trajectory can be tweaked to empower us to reconnect with our feelings and intuition. As an ex award-winning Army commando and national sporting champion, I am not about to go all woo-woo on you, but I will ask you to consider the words of American author Michael Neill from his book *The Inside Out Revolution*, 'We're only ever one thought away from a completely different experience of life.'

What needs to change

It's time to build a life beyond the old blueprint. We need to talk more expressively, and to communicate more readily, openly and authentically. This is what it means to be human. For this to happen, men need to learn how to interpret their feelings and, equally, feel safe expressing and communicating them.

Think about it. Currently, the only socially acceptable 'safe' space for men to express emotion among other men is in sport, whether that's watching or playing. In sport, we cry with joy when our team lifts the cup or get publicly angry when our team throws the game. That needs to change. We need to be able to express our feelings beyond the world of sports in our marriages, our friendships and our relationships with our children.

It's hard; I get it and I empathise with that. We've spent our whole lives being told to 'man up', but that's more dangerous than we've been led to believe. As Sigmund Freud said, 'Unexpressed emotions will never die. They are buried alive and will come forth later in uglier ways.'

To emphasise Freud's (and my) point, I'll illustrate it with a metaphor you will most likely be familiar with. Imagine that you're in a swimming pool, hiding an inflatable ball under the water. That ball is full of your suppressed and repressed feelings. Your whole life is in that ball: the parts of you you've tried to hide; the unwanted experiences you've encountered; the aspects of your life that cause you shame, anger, sadness and embarrassment. As you journey through life, the ball continues to inflate.

Inevitably, the act of emotional suppression will cause fatigue and become tiresome. You'll struggle to keep the ball under the water, pushing it down, hiding it from public view. One day, the ball will get so full or you'll grow so tired, you won't be able to defy its buoyancy or control it. It will burst out of the water with its years of repressed energy. It's going to hit you in the face and make a splash in your life.

Like it did with me.

In 2017, it was five years since I had left my successful military career and I had recently become a father for the first time. When I took off my uniform, I also – unknowingly at the time – lost my sense of identity and purpose. Not knowing who I was and what I wanted my life to stand for, compounded by the stresses of first-time fatherhood, created a perfect (shit)storm in my life.

For months, I was secretly suffering, trapped in my own thoughts, sometimes anxious, other times depressed. While no one recognised it at the time, I was in the freefall stage of an identity crisis, but I hid it all away behind my perfected nice-guy persona and my 'it's weak to speak' mask.

Then, I let go of everything I'd been trying to hide beneath the surface of my life and repress in my own psyche. I took my hands off 'the ball' and pressed self-destruct on my entire life. I left my wife. I blamed her for 'breaking me', but in hindsight, I was already broken. I was trying to live a life I didn't understand. It was a messy and painful chapter for both me and my wife. What had happened to the man she married?

This was the start of something, a recalibration of who I am and what I stand for. I'll explain later in the book exactly what sparked the moment of realisation, but for now, know this: I learned the importance of stopping negative self-talk. I learned how to express my feelings and prioritise my own happiness, and this benefited everyone around me, including my wife. I was able to build a new marriage with her: one that is based on shared life goals, authenticity and connection. I now have a clear future image of myself, the life I will lead and the legacy I want to leave behind. My recalibration changed my life.

You too can create a life with a clear future image of yourself, and then develop the habits that underpin who you aspire to become. With self-reflection, self-awareness and self-leadership, you'll tune back into your intuition, see the value in small things and prioritise your wellbeing. No more pretending. No more putting on a show to appease others.

REFLECTION EXERCISES

- When you reflect back, what was the moment or period of your life where you feel you became a man?

- When you consider becoming a man, who were the men that taught you how to do it?

- What skills, traits, qualities did they teach and pass on to you?

- Look back over your life to this point. In addition to what they did teach you, what else do you wish they had passed on?

- From a societal perspective, what do you feel we as men are currently teaching our children about masculinity and the wider world?

- If you can only teach your children one thing to equip them for the complexities of life, what would you teach them and why?

3

Middle-aged Mediocrity

Did you know that the least happy and most anxious men in the population are those aged forty to fifty-nine?[1] Around this time, life goes from being an engaging ride to a potentially meaningless shuffle. Life, work, family, friendships and health can feel average at best, and that is what I call middle-aged mediocrity.

The truth is, many men simply settle into complacency around middle age. Exercise and fitness drop down the priority list and before they know it, they're saddled with a 'dad bod'. Work is all-encompassing and they start every day by habitually checking their emails with a sense of dread. Time for family and hobbies is scarce; middle-aged men often say they put family first, but the reality is family comes second.

What happens to the striving attitude and purpose of our twenties and thirties? It dissipates and goes, it seems. In middle age, this tends to be reflected back at us everywhere we go. We switch on *Peppa Pig* for the children and see Daddy Pig struggling to put pictures up on the wall, always out of breath. We switch to *The Simpsons* and there's Homer, drinking away his boredom from work at Moe's tavern. There's humour in these shows, but they reflect a real side of masculinity today as they're the fruit of intergenerational messaging that has planted subconscious seeds about what it means to be a man. The result is that many middle-aged men are now just bumbling through life.

How could they not? They've often been pulled in so many different directions all their life, they've lost their sense of identity and purpose. They find themselves simply paying lip service to life, going through the motions. They're saddled with feelings of inadequacy, uncertainty and guilt, but too many of them don't feel there's anything they can do about it.

I used to hear my wife talk about mum guilt when leaving the children, but what about dad guilt? Many middle-aged men are watching themselves become the dads they never wanted to be, but they're unable to stop the momentum they've built up in this direction. They recognise that their life isn't what they expected and wanted it to be, but they're too afraid to speak up, worried that it might make them seem inferior to others. It's no wonder that many middle-aged men are stuck in a rut of mediocrity.

THE GAME OF LIFE

We've mentioned the game of life briefly before, but now let's look at the expectations and rules of a successful life for a modern man.

Sport is a great metaphor for life. Just like sport, life consists of levels, and the more you earn, the higher the level you play at. Going level to level, though – buying the new car, the nice house and speeding ahead in the rat race, key stages in the game of life – will only make you unhappy. The system funnels men into the trap of mediocrity, whether they like it or not, and it starts with societal priorities at each stage of the game of life.

The pre-conditioned priorities are clear in **adolescence**, where we are programmed to focus on competing, whether it's in sports, academically or for the attention of girls (this pre-conditioning makes no allowances for any option other than heterosexuality). Then, in our **twenties**, it's all about having a disposable income and living a lifestyle level with or above that of our peers. In our **thirties**, we're told to make sacrifices, striving to do well in our career, get married and start a family. For the **forty-somethings**, it's buying the big forever home and collecting the symbols of success. In our **fifties**, we're conditioned to prioritise living life through our children's successes and posting pictures of our fantastic holidays. Finally, in our **sixties and beyond**, we enjoy the perfect retirement and show off our grandchildren.

It's all planned out in advance in the game of life, but the fact is, most people who play this way lose. Bronnie Ware, an Australian palliative care nurse, showed this better than I ever could.[2] She interviewed people as they were literally on their deathbed and recorded the top five regrets of her dying patients over the years. They had no reason to pretend their life had been something it wasn't, as their game of life was nearly up. The results might be uncomfortable for you to read.

- **Regret 1:** Not having the courage to live a life true to myself.
- **Regret 2:** Working too hard.
- **Regret 3:** Not having the courage to express my feelings.
- **Regret 4:** Not staying in touch with my friends.
- **Regret 5:** Not letting myself be happier.

As these regrets clearly show us, although almost all successful middle-aged men have played the game of life 'by the rules', they're still going to lose. Take regret #2, for example. Isn't working hard the way to success? Most men already know they work too hard, but they justify it by telling themselves that they are doing it for their families while the truth hides in plain sight: the game of life is not fulfilling.

Sadly, I've attended a few funerals lately and seen friends and family close to me contend with this stark realisation. Suddenly, the fleeting nature of life is all they can think about. They want to be less stressed and more present, but they aren't ready to give themselves permission to do so. As the pain of bereavement passes, they are sucked back into their own mediocrity, playing the game of life.

Comparison with other players

This is a key component of the game of life. Think back to Chapter 2 as the role of post-war fatherhood becomes relevant here once again. These men came home and wanted a humble life. A quiet life. Their sons grew up and wanted more, creating a culture of 'keeping up with the Joneses'. Men would compare their houses, cars, wives and families with their neighbours' as a benchmark for their own success.

As a result, the stereotypical successful man to this day has an ongoing desire for newer, bigger or better cars than his neighbours and is busy comparing golf clubs before tee off with his friends and connections. Meanwhile, his wife is measuring up the family holidays against those her friends have enjoyed, his children want the latest clothes for school and everyone in the family 'needs' the latest smart phone. Everyone's living in a constant state of comparison.

Can you guess what's made this even worse? Social media. It's not about keeping up with the Joneses anymore. Now, we're keeping up with the whole world. Selecting certain images that portray exactly how we want to come across, we can build up a digital version of ourselves. The problem with that? We grow to fit the mask we wear and this gives us a false sense of who we are, and who others are, too.

On average, people spend 145 minutes every day on social media.[3] That's a lot of time to compare ourselves to others and it leaves a lasting mark. In one survey, 62% of respondents stated that their self-esteem had been impacted in a negative way by social-media use.[4]

We have been conditioned to believe that holidays, cars and houses are the metrics of success. The items, experiences and possessions that were once viewed as luxurious have now, because of clever and targeted advertising, seemingly become necessities. Our 'need' for these items serves to heighten our dependency on money and compound our experience of the rat-race lifestyle. We find ourselves with a constant yearning for more. All for just a fleeting boost of serotonin on the hedonic treadmill.

Soon, we're right back to where we started, because this is the truth of it: our happiness has an underlying set point that it will fall back to time and time again, no matter how much we buy. Science tells us that genetics make up an estimated 40% of our ability to be happy,[5] but what about that other 60%?

We have more control over our happiness than we may have been led to believe. That 60% is made up of life satisfaction, feeling engaged, having a sense of purpose (something we'll explore in Chapter 7) and the quality of our relationships. Purchasing a new car is noticeably absent from the list.

Social media plants subconscious seeds of envy and triggers feelings of insignificance and self-doubt. The messages we see on social media are then reinforced by popular culture. We switch on Netflix or Amazon Prime and see shows where perfect families live perfect lives in warm climates. How are we ever meant to appreciate what we have when we're constantly being told we can have more, go bigger, do better?

This problem goes beyond our phone and TV screen, too. In Sao Paolo, Brazil, billboard advertising was banned and instead replaced with works of art when the city planners recognised the unconscious conditioning that was happening and understood that this reinforcement was dangerous.[6] 70% of residents said the change made Sao Paolo a better city to live in. Sweden and Greece also banned advertising directed at children. This shows that we as human beings are clearly aware of the problem, but because we're here in the game of life, we're stuck with it.

THE MESSY MIDDLE

Where are you in the game of life right now? Are you feeling stuck in the average, mediocre and messy middle section of the game? This is defined by being time poor and lost in the responsibilities of work, career and community, which leaves little time and energy for yourself and your own identity.

Because of the pressures associated with the messy middle, many men subconsciously dilute themselves and give up on all the things that made them who they are. Going the gym or keeping fit; playing eighteen holes of golf; enjoying an annual ski trip; even going to gigs or attending sporting events becomes a rarity. These men are almost always connected online, but disconnected physically. Sadly, at a deep level they know it, they feel it, but they don't know how or what to do to break free.

How does this happen? Think about it. It's 'normal' and it's easy to become the norm.

Your career in the messy middle

Work usually defines the lives of my clients when they first come to me. They leave the house before their partner or family wakes up. They eat an unsatisfying breakfast on the commute, and then settle down at the office for a day in front of the computer. Their only break is going to the toilet. They say they'll finish at five, but stay on until six before heading home. Those who have children, if they manage to see them before they go to bed, it's quick. When the children are in bed, these men will spend thirty minutes with their partner, and then work from their smart phone or home office. They go to bed when everyone else in the household is asleep, and then they'll do it all again tomorrow.

The game of life gives us less reward for this than we may think. Many men spend their lives pushing themselves, working day in and day out to get that promotion, but once they get there, they realise it isn't all it's cracked up to be. This is the paradox of promotion. They have to work harder and prove themselves all over again. It's never ending, but that's the game of life. We climb the ladder – but we need to be careful it's against the right wall.

Feelings in the messy middle

As we've established, men have been taught to suppress the caring, more vulnerable elements of their masculinity by the time they reach middle age, so many men by this point feel numb to the world and disconnected. Their masculinity has become toxic to themselves, others and the world at large, but watch any man with his newborn and you'll realise that his caring side is still there.

The constructs of masculinity force us as men to act in a certain way: emotionless, in control and courageous. With our children, or even our siblings' or friends' children, we can be nurturing, kind and compassionate. That side of masculinity is within us all, but we are forced to fight against it every day, throwing us out of balance with ourselves and the world around us.

My clients often struggle with realising the problems and challenges they are experiencing are not unique to them; many other men are experiencing the exact same things, but because they get stuck in their heads, marinating themselves in their own negative thinking, they don't realise these issues aren't personal, they're societal. The shocking numbers of men experiencing burnout, loneliness, poor mental health, midlife crisis and divorce only serve to highlight this.

This is exactly why I call these men the silent majority – suffering without ever sharing the discomfort or their reality. It's the myth of masculinity that keeps them trapped, lonely and feeling like nobody understands them. Does this resonate with you? Believe me when I say you're not alone.

Fatherhood In the messy middle

Fatherhood can feel like a sucker punch and, despite the nine-month warning, it can turn our lives upside down. Of course, everyone tells us it'll be hard and we hear about the sleepless nights, but new dads will rarely tell their friends and families about how hard it really is, what it actually feels like.

As much as those of us who are fathers love our children, the first years can be thankless and, at times, relentless. The reality is, fatherhood triggers guilt around working too much in the messy middle. We're stuck between a rock and a hard place as the main earner and the father, which can create a sense of resentment, feeling like we're working two jobs: one, our pressurised career position, the other, our new parental responsibilities.

Studies have shown that 67% of couples report a decline in relationship satisfaction after the arrival of the first baby.[7] This is reflected across many men's lives as they simply find themselves unable to cope with the new expectations and feelings brought up by the change to their family dynamic.

I have met men who park around the corner from their houses and call their wives to see if it sounds chaotic at home. If it does, they'll do another thirty minutes of work in the car, avoiding the situation at home. They feel it is too much after a full day of work to be expected to take on parental responsibilities. This causes distance between couples that can lead to their separation – all because these men aren't accepting and expressing how they are feeling about the situation.

Fatherhood, particularly for the first time, is tough. Then later in parenthood, there's a fresh challenge. As a child's personality develops, many dads find themselves wanting to be home more, but being unable to. There's a sense of being pulled in two directions: not wanting to miss out, but also not being able to earn enough money to support the family if they spend too much time with the children. Fatherhood in the messy middle is a cause of real stress.

Internal narrative in the messy middle

In the messy middle, our internal narrative is defined by inner conflict. Our subconscious mind is telling us one thing – constructed mostly from conditioning and the meaning we give to past personal experiences. This includes everything that others tell us or teach us about ourselves, but we also feel that what we have been taught isn't quite right. We feel a sense of our lives not being good enough, of not having the answers to the questions in our own mind.

Think about the narrative that men have been sold so far. Right now, you may be telling yourself that time is money, or that your relationship can be reduced to happy wife = happy life. That probably doesn't feel quite right, but it's hard to break free from that story; it's hard to push past the conflict and be your true self, because your true self may be 'different' from the rest.

The unforgiving playground taught us all the extra-curricular lesson that we can be anything we want to be, but we can't be different. As a result, at school, we learned to shed our uniqueness and fit the masculine mould.

I did a quick poll on LinkedIn recently to dive further into this. I asked men what the 'worst' thing they could be in school was. The results illuminated the same sadly unsurprising trends. Overall, being gay or having any other characteristics deemed by immature and adolescent boys to be 'feminine' was seen as the 'worst'. Things got even more interesting when I looked into the comments section. Men mentioned the stigma attached to being seen as a mummy's boy. To summarise the unsurprising – anything associated with boys having feminine traits was severely looked down upon at school.

With many young boys not sure how to be a man and having no purpose-driven and openly expressive male role models, the playground mentality shapes their view of their own masculinity. Being too different, too feminine, too wimpy, too fat, too ginger – these are all things that are simply unique parts of who children are, but we are taught to hide and suppress them in our formative years. Then, we grow up and enter the world of work where, in many corporate organisations and at the sharp edge of business, it's a case of fit in or f*ck off. In our careers, toxic masculinity turns us into the corporate alpha male, the rat-race specialist.

As a caveat here, masculinity in itself isn't toxic. It's powerful and protective, but in its current form, it's dysfunctional.

What we weren't taught

If nothing changes, nothing changes. Where do you see yourself in ten years' time if nothing changes? Sure, you'll be a decade older, but what many of us fail to comprehend is that the man we see in the mirror today is creating the man that we will be tomorrow – and in ten years' time. Applying old learnings from outdated models just won't cut it anymore. It's time to think about what nobody explicitly ever teaches us, which are exactly the practical principles that enable us to succeed in life:

- How to manage our mindset
- How to communicate effectively
- How to think critically and objectively
- How to formulate plans and make decisions
- How to interpret and regulate our emotions
- How to build and maintain healthy relationships

Most of us as boys copied and role modelled our fathers or those in influential positions, and those people were likely following the old blueprint of masculinity that we now know isn't serving the men of our era. Masculinity in its current form is restrictive and controlling for men. We experience inner conflict, which leads to inner confusion, but instead of talking about it, we fall into unhealthy patterns to help us 'deal with it'.

Through my coaching, I've identified three core ways that men deal with difficulties:

- They 'numb it out', avoiding their emotions and eventually becoming numb to them.
- They 'nice it out', getting caught in the trap of appeasing others and people pleasing.
- They 'act it out', creating an outwardly obvious explosion of emotion – an aggressive form of self-sabotage.

These patterns become a part of who we are. Take a moment to consider the three options of numb it out, nice it out or act it out. Which is your most common trait? Are you detached, a pushover or do you blow your lid at the slightest provocation?

Until recently, most of us had our heads down and were plodding along in whichever pattern we felt fitted us best, but the COVID-19 pandemic changed everything. It brought about a fundamental shift in the way we work, connect and spend our time.

THE LOCKDOWN EFFECT

Not wanting to sound cold or callous, I genuinely believe that the COVID lockdowns were a wake-up call the world didn't know it needed. They paused the game of life, and in the wake of the game being paused, many people looked around and registered that they really weren't all that happy. Without the frantic pace of life and constant distractions pulling them in a million different directions, they discovered the disconnection they had within themselves and with those 'closest' to them. It was almost a 'How have I ended up here?' moment for a significant percentage of the professionally successful population.

Divorce enquiries went up, and so did the number of people feeling burned out. People sought real, meaningful work and connection with others. Zoom quizzes became incredibly popular as people tried to pay more attention to those they now realised they missed. For many, their perspective on life fundamentally changed.

When we change the way we look at things, the things we look at change, and that's what happened during lockdown. Our social media feeds post-COVID tended to be a constant stream of weddings, engagements, new babies, career announcements and keys held happily outside newly purchased homes: big, meaningful life events that became more frequent now than they had ever been before as people re-prioritised and re-engaged in their busy lives.

One poll found that 22% of adults either moved house or town because of the pandemic, or knew someone who did.[8] About 20% more houses sold in November 2020 than in November 2019.[9] This perspective shift didn't go anywhere after lockdown: post-COVID, people resigned from their careers in droves, in a trend that has been dubbed the 'Great Resignation'.[10] All around the world, people are realising that they are not happy with their careers or their lives and are making significant changes.

What about the shift in our mentality? The number of dads out on their bikes with their children, walking the dog and gaining headspace increased significantly in the pandemic. This has made many of my clients realise that they need more time with their families – not the work-life-balance part-time kind, but real, meaningful and purposeful time. Why? Because it feels good. It's natural for men to spend time with their families and connect and bond. It's unnatural to be distant and disconnected.

Pre-pandemic, men were known to suffer in silence, rarely reaching out for help. After the pandemic, things changed. Men were given permission to talk, to ask for support and to open up about their feelings. A national counselling helpline specifically for men reported a 95% increase in calls about mental health post-pandemic. Calls about relationships also increased by 36%.[11] While the stress of the pandemic probably caused these calls, it also enabled these men to reach out and get the help they needed – something they likely would not have done without the fundamental societal shifts of the lockdowns.

When men give themselves permission to talk about their feelings, great things happen and they connect with themselves and their loved ones on a deeper level than before. I've seen significant changes to men's ability to talk through their challenges in my Men & Mountains group, and I've seen these men grow as people accordingly. With the pandemic, I experienced an increase in enquiries to join the group, showing me that men are ready to reach out for the support they need.

This is a step in the right direction. An antidote to depression is expression. When you express, you release and reduce the feeling of self-imposed isolation we discussed earlier.

What this means for you

Let's own where we're at and muster the courage to disrupt what it means to experience the world as a man. It is our time to make the changes we want to see in the world. It is our chance to be the generations of men who course-correct and craft an entirely new blueprint of masculinity to hand down to our sons.

I want to leave the old gender stereotypes behind and redefine masculinity as being self-aware, purpose-driven, emotionally expressive leaders of ourselves. This will enhance the life experience of our generations and generations to come. We have the power to change the benchmark and yardstick by which we measure masculinity, but it must be a collective effort; we must work together.

That starts with you. You now have a greater understanding of the problems of modern masculinity and how these have shaped the world you were born into and guided your life's journey. It's time to take control and make a positive change to your life. It's time to lead yourself and craft your legacy.

The next few chapters will help you to truly live your life. You'll learn about the anti-values that define your life right now and the BetterMen blueprint that you will aim to achieve. You'll discover the path to self-leadership and to living with intention.

Read on to make the base camp for the next stage of your life. It's time to live beyond the narrow and restrictive version of masculinity we've all been given.

REFLECTION EXERCISES

- Why do you feel so many professionally successful men live personally unhappy lives?

- Having heard the top five regrets of the dying, at this juncture in your life, what do you regret about the things you have and haven't done?

- In the game of life, we constantly compare. When you notice yourself comparing yourself to other men, what are you comparing yourself against?

- Nothing compounds the messy middle like becoming a dad. If you're a father, in what ways did fatherhood change you, your relationship, your life?

- Personal sacrifice is common in the messy middle. What things did you once enjoy doing that now, for whatever reason, you no longer do?

- If COVID really was 'the wake up the world didn't know it needed', what realities or changes did the lockdowns wake you up to?

PART TWO

THE CROSSROADS OF MASCULINITY

4

No Man's Land

Welcome to Part 2 of this book. Here, we won't allow ourselves to numb or avoid the hard truths we discussed in Part 1; instead, we will focus our effort on laying the foundations for both rethinking masculinity and implementing the meaningful changes that will improve our experience of life.

Perhaps certain elements of masculinity in Part 1 resonated with you, sparking reflection or making you uncomfortable. Please understand, it's not your fault that you followed this path – you were conditioned to believe it was the right thing to do.

From my own experience and that of many of my clients, I've learned that there are three psychological states to a man's journey: *asleep*, *aware* and *awake*. You may have been *asleep* throughout most of your life, running on autopilot, playing the game of life. Recently, you've possibly been feeling a little more *aware*. Perhaps you've had a subtle sense of dissatisfaction and you're questioning your life's decisions and direction.

Finally, there's *awake*. This is where you want to be: it means you're in the driver's seat, consciously influencing everything you experience and leading yourself forward to where you want to go.

You really can build the life you want, but you need to understand what it means to be aware before you can shift to awake. Perhaps you recognise that you're lacking meaningful goals, a strong sense of purpose and the depth of connection that you want, realising there must be more to life. Perhaps you're secretly uncomfortable and frustrated with the life you're living. That innate discomfort you're feeling is a message and even at this early stage of our journey together, I'd advise you to listen to it – it's your true self calling for change.

Wartime Prime Minister Winston Churchill said, 'Men occasionally stumble over the truth, but most of them pick themselves up and hurry off as if nothing had happened.' The chapters in Part 2 will teach you to rise above the men scurrying back to pre-pandemic normality, face your truth and change your life in intentional ways. They will teach you what it means to be aware, so that you can move in Part 3 to being awake.

Now let's dive into understanding the transitional state of being aware. If you're familiar with the film, consider the scene from *The Matrix* where Neo is offered the choice between the blue and the red pill. The blue pill is your old life, following the old blueprint and doing what you've always done. The red pill is a new life – one where you follow the healthier blueprint of masculinity, defined by self-awareness, purpose and expression.

THE SIGNS OF NO MAN'S LAND

When you're *aware* that you're unhappy with your life, but feel unable to change it, you're in no man's land. Many men at this stage think that because they're professionally successful, everything should be fine, but they know it's not. They're stuck in their story, going around in circles. Where they are is not where they want to be.

Neither owning how they feel nor acting upon their feelings, on autopilot, they're just plodding along, doing more of what they've done in the past, even though it's leading them to a tiresome and potentially unfulfilling future. The game of life has taught them that if they tick certain boxes, they should feel happy, but it hasn't worked – and there's the issue. More of the same isn't what they need.

These men don't want to go back to the way things were, but they also don't know how to move forward, so they're in no man's land. Unfortunately, no man's land is the most dangerous place to be.

Men who stay in no man's land lose their sense of identity and dilute their purpose. Over time, they slip into an apathetic state. While they know this isn't what they want for their lives, they don't invest the time to consider what they might want instead. They're stuck. The gap between knowing and acting can prove costly, often with a man's happiness being paid as the ultimate price.

Being stuck in no man's land creates conflict within ourselves. It affects the way we show up and interact with the world around us and inevitably proves detrimental in our most precious relationships.

In this section, we will look at some of the signs of a man stuck in no man's land.

Work/life conflict

Work is mentally, emotionally and physically consuming and a locked-out, pressurised diary creeps into time that was once reserved for family togetherness. Unhappiness with being in the rat race and feelings of stress caused by the pressures of being the provider can lead to a man having a foggy, detached mindset at home. It's hard to bring his 'real self' to life outside of work because he can't quite connect with who that is anymore. Work consumes his life and his individuality, causing detachment both personally and in relationships.

Dad guilt

No man's land is rife with dad guilt. Many men here feel pulled in all directions – they're being required to perform at work and show up as engaged, proactive fathers. They're consumed with guilt as they can't give 100% of their energy to their children and home life as well as 100% at work. It feels like they're stuck between a rock and a hard place – these dads need to provide financially, but it comes at the cost of being mentally present and emotionally connected at home.

Unhappiness

For a man in no man's land, unhappiness in one area of his life will infect the other areas. Snappiness and irritability after a long day at the office can lead to frustration and resentment towards himself and his life, with patience in short supply.

Furthermore, men in no man's land feel adrift from real purpose, with no tangible goals. When someone's lacking a sense of purpose without moving towards meaningful goals, they become disillusioned or easily distracted.

Insecurity

In no man's land, comparison is everything. As we explored in previous chapters, social media and keeping up with the Joneses lead to a constant feeling of inadequacy, of not being 'enough', but what is 'enough-ness'? The idea of being successful enough, smart enough, man enough, physically fit enough, of achieving enough... these concepts devalue a man's personal achievements and corrode his self-esteem.

Avoidance

The discomfort and frustration of living in no man's land is ever present, but the characteristic response here is simply to 'avoid'. Avoid the reality; avoid the confrontation; avoid the discomfort of the truth.

When we try to avoid our reality, we mostly make things worse. In the case of getting out of no man's land, we need to make conscious changes if we want to turn things around. Just take a look at the world of physics – paraphrasing Newton's first law of motion, an object at rest will remain at rest unless it is acted upon by a force. We need to act!

How did any of us arrive in no man's land? We followed the old blueprint for masculine success passed down by our fathers and grandfathers – men whose definition of success was different to ours. In doing so, we've become strong and silent and have made many personal sacrifices to achieve professionally, but now we're there, it isn't all it's cracked up to be.

Perhaps you're starting to see the myth of masculinity for what it is: a flawed way to live life.

SUCCESS WITHOUT FULFILMENT

In no man's land, an incredible number of men have the material trappings of success, but lack the happiness and fulfilment they expected to accompany it. The myth of masculinity led them here and what a mess it can create. From my conversations with clients, I know there are many professional men who can't even enjoy going on holiday. The emails pile up, the things pending approval stay pending until their return.

If this resonates with you, you have to ask yourself what type of life are you living if you can't take a holiday without burying yourself in work beforehand or dreading your return?

No man's land offers unfulfilling work

Many of us have spent years of our lives grabbing a cup of coffee at work, raising it in jest to our colleagues and saying, 'Well, back to the grind.' Think about that for a second. To grind means rubbing something with enough force to break it. The boredom, the fatigue, the pressure are all breaking you into tiny pieces, and it's likely you know it. If you've ever said that you're going back to the grind, you even joke about it. As always, the truth is hidden in plain sight.

Professional success does not equal happiness. It never has, it never will. Men all around the world are unfulfilled, with only 15% reporting that they feel engaged at work, despite having achieved nothing but success on paper.[1] Going fast and working hard while still heading in the wrong direction is a flawed approach. The psychological impact of success without fulfilment is real: inner confusion creating inner conflict.

As we have discussed, it seems that men are taught to lose their sense of self, connection and community in social media and buy their way to happiness. The truth is, social media can't compensate us psychologically for what we have lost. Despite many a man's best efforts, we can't buy our way out of unhappiness and we can't hustle our way into happiness – happiness is a state where a man feels a deep sense of connection; where he's living in alignment and is creating the life he wants to live. None of us will ever achieve that state when we're constantly struggling against the weight of expectation we place on ourselves.

Trust me. If this resonates with you, you're not alone. Men all around the world are putting heavy expectations on themselves, locking themselves in boxes. One study showed that 49% of men believe that they are expected to figure out their personal problems alone, while 47% stated that a man must always act strong even if he's terrified inside.[2] That's no way to live. You know it, I know it. Now it's time to do something about it.

The anti-climax of achievement

Sometimes, achieving our goals can be an anti-climax. I have clients who sold their businesses for six-, seven- and eight-figure sums with the expectation that they would feel a sense of deep fulfilment, only to be left feeling short-changed by their success. Others landed their dream job, but were disappointed to see that it swiftly became a nightmare. It was everything they thought it would be, but it also came with significant unexpected pressure and the weight of extra expectation.

Sadly, this seems somewhat normal. Consider the Olympic athlete. They spend years building up to the Olympic Games. Their lives are defined by reaching their highest possible performance, but what about when it's all over? Many feel lost. American swimmer Michael Phelps, for example, described falling into a depression after the London Olympics.[3] Similarly, in professional sport, England rugby star Jonny Wilkinson described himself as 'feeling empty' in the aftermath of 2003 Rugby World Cup glory.[4]

Through my work, I've discovered that there really is no difference between the corporate space, high-level sport and the military. They're all strong masculine cultures, following the old blueprint. I'm sure you know what I mean – the harder you work, the more you're paid, promoted or recognised. Whoever sacrifices the most 'life' climbs the corporate ladder the fastest and goes the furthest.

We're expected to or we expect ourselves to achieve peak performance in our career or business, and so we do. Many of my clients have reached the pinnacle of their profession, but then, like the successful Olympians and Rugby World Cup winners, they feel lost. They either go on to set the bar of attainment even higher (trapping and grinding themselves down further) or keep going and stay too long in their role because they don't know who they'd be outside of their 'arena'.

It's not all doom and gloom in this section, though. One way I have found to bypass this trap and reach significance in your life is philanthropy: using your skills and resources for charitable causes.

The life quake

Some clients come to me because they've had a life quake during their sprint to their Olympic levels of performance. What's a life quake? It can be presented in many ways: their marriage may be falling apart; they may have been promoted beyond what they feel they're capable of; they may be struggling to be an active parent; maybe they've had a health scare or experienced the pain of a close bereavement. The form it takes is irrelevant; what matters is that life has shaken them and woken them up. They've become *aware* they need to sort aspects of their life out.

An unfulfilling retirement

Let's talk briefly about where you'll end up if you choose to stay trapped in no man's land, aware that you're unhappy, but doing nothing about it. You'll end up retired, which on the surface, because of our societal conditioning, doesn't sound too bad, does it? Unfortunately, for many men, retirement proves to be another unfulfilling chapter of life.

Men are meant to keep their nose to the grindstone for four decades and then stop, look up and be rewarded with the time to do everything they want, but that just leads to more unhappiness. The rate of retirees reporting that they are completely unhappy with their retirement is 10%.[5] The number of people who are only moderately satisfied is staggeringly low at 40.9%. Combined, that means that 50.9% of retirees, essentially half of the people who've hung on for retirement, don't enjoy it. I don't know about you, but that seems like a huge life risk to me.

Just like the myth of masculinity, the promise of an idyllic life in the last chapter of a man's journey is also a lie. Retired men aren't happy.

Studies show that male retirees drink more than women, live more sedentary lifestyles, have fewer social interactions and smoke more.[6] A 2021 report from the World Health Organization states that long working hours increases the likelihood of people dying prematurely of heart disease and stroke, and that this has primarily affected men (72% of deaths).[7]

The average life expectancy for a man in the UK is seventy-nine years.[8] Think about that. It means you get seventy-nine laps around the sun and you're meant to wait to start living your life until you've hit sixty-five. Perhaps an unhappy and unfulfilling life at that. Something's not right. If you're reading this and recognise you're in no man's land, you really do need to get out of it!

THE ANTI-VALUES

My clients typically come to me in one of three states: feeling dissatisfied and directionless (secretly unhappy with their unfulfilling lives); in fight-or-flight mode (experiencing some kind of warning tremor or life quake); or because they are so lonely at the top that they need an unbiased sounding board or confidant (a safe space to decompress and address their imbalances).

At the time of writing this book, I've worked with hundreds of men over thousands of hours of conversation and coaching. Through the process of my work, I have collated what I call the anti-values. These create the day-to-day state of modern masculinity and stand in opposition to the BetterMen values, which I will present in the last part of the book.

The anti-values are what we aim to move away from. The BetterMen values are what we aspire to move towards.

Life in no man's land is defined by these six anti-values. Read through and see which resonate with you.

- **Capacity:** we're constantly running at maximum capacity. Our mental tabs are always open; we have no time, space or energy for anything, especially not ourselves. We can't slow down or switch off.

- **Comfort:** being too comfortable for too long can be corrosive. When we've bought the nice house and the big car and have ticked life's boxes, staying in this state without setting new fulfilling goals leads to boredom.

- **Conformity:** we think that because everyone else is living life 'this' way and buying 'these' things, we should too, so we enthusiastically participate in the game of life and its destructive cousin, the rat race.

- **Complacency:** with no sense of purpose, we'll drift through life. We won't consciously notice the absence of goals or lack of drive that once inspired us; instead, we may just notice the dullness of our lives.

- **Communication:** internally, because we don't listen to our intuition or feelings, we don't understand ourselves. Externally, we feel there's no 'safe' space to talk, so we don't – we bottle everything up.

- **Certainty:** perhaps the most serious anti-value. We're so certain there'll be a pot of gold at the end of the rainbow, we're set in our ways, living a blinkered life with a closed-minded approach.

Do any of these anti-values resonate with you? Do they feel like accurate descriptions of your life? I wouldn't be surprised – they're common side effects of following the old blueprint of masculinity. It's making good quality men like you and me miserable in our own lives.

MEN ARE IGNORING THE WARNING SIGNS

The system is clearly not working as we expect. Many men are aware that they're unhappy, but lack the capacity to communicate their situation, to let go of their certainty and complacency and break free of their conformity and comfort. Why has nobody stood up and done something about it? We're told as men to be strong – why has nobody used their strength to tear down the whole broken system?

Because it's normal. We're taught to ignore the warning signs. We're taught to stick silently to the path because we believe it to be 'safe' to do so, but in reality, what we think creates safety keeps us small and isolated. By staying in our lane of life, we will likely arrive at destination despair without ever exposing ourselves to new challenges, new opportunities and a new way of living.

When men that live life from the anti-values feel threatened by change or notice they're not happy, they'll wish things were different or they'll resist the change in the hope of regaining the status quo. Let's explore why.

The iceberg of masculinity

Statistically speaking, 87% of an iceberg is hidden beneath the water. Masculinity is much like an iceberg: the majority of what makes a man is hidden. Above the water, we have the 'traditionally masculine' traits, and underneath it an abundance of human traits. Many men seem in control, confident and certain, but below the water, we're questioning who we are and what we want. We're wondering, 'How did I arrive here?', 'What do I stand for?' and 'What does my life represent?'

We're so used to operating from the tip of the iceberg that we ignore warning signs below the surface. For many men, there's nothing to see and everything to feel, but we wear the mask of masculinity to protect ourselves from feeling those feelings. As novelist George Orwell said, 'He wears a mask and his face grows to fit it.'[9] This is a dangerous strategy; ignoring our feelings can result in us becoming numb to ourselves and life, which compounds our problems.

Have you noticed that day to day, we as men tend to mask our feelings to keep the peace, appease others and fit in? We hide our real selves to maintain the balance of our 'perfect lives', so when those intuitive feelings that tell us that everything isn't OK come creeping in, we ignore them. We push them away. Not just you and not just me, but millions of men all over the world do this, which is what has left us where we are today.

The dangers of ignoring the warning signs

The dangers of ignoring the warning signs of being in no man's land are real. You'll find yourself sleepwalking through life, wasting more of your precious laps around the sun. Despite your best efforts, you can't ignore the warning signs; they're innate messages. When you disregard them, you create unhelpful habits – both consciously and subconsciously – to mitigate how you're really feeling.

The subconscious mind is powerful. It creates shortcuts and habitual patterns which influence behaviour more than you may think. You've likely fallen into thought patterns that you didn't even realise you had. One of those may be automatic negative thoughts (ANTs).

Here's what ANTs may look like:

- You find you're always thinking
- You tend to focus on the negative
- You hear yourself frequently saying I should, I must
- You label – I am lazy; I am not good enough; I am a failure
- You tend to predict the future, largely the worst outcomes
- You find that you're often defensive and you demonstrate this through blaming others

Whenever you're faced with the opportunity to make a change – to shift from *aware* to *awake* – you'll likely fall back on those ANTs. They are controlling your thinking and therefore your life. Ignoring the warning signs of your unhappiness could be practically an automatic process at this point.

Many of my clients who are stuck in this state come to me with issues such as procrastination, rumination, analysis paralysis, irritability, suppressed anger, sadness, presentism and apathy. All of these are controlled by their own subconscious and conscious minds.

Life doesn't have to be this way. We don't need to continue being overwhelmed by work and responsibilities and underwhelmed by everything else.

BREAKING DOWN FEAR AND SELF-RESISTANCE

Now that the measuring stick of 'successful masculinity' is changing, there's a chance to build and become something more. I believe that modern men are able to find a path beyond pursuing material success, instead achieving a deeper sense of fulfilment and freedom. You are the cause and effect of everything you experience – so choose to cause change.

Creating change starts with breaking down fear and self-resistance. We cling tightly to the habits, patterns and themes (like the ANTs) that define our lives. When we allow ourselves to let go of the patterns, the themes that aren't supporting us, we can choose a different path and forge a better way ahead, but we need to be aware that there's something standing in our way: fear. We need to dismantle that to move forward.

We are born with only two fears: the fear of falling and the fear of loud noises,[10] so what happens throughout our lives to create so many more? The way I see it is this – we can get trapped in our heads, imagining the negative consequences of the things that could go wrong, particularly so if we're struggling with low self-worth or viewing life through a lens of anxiety. However, fears are just thoughts.

Read that again: *fear is just a thought.*

We have so many thoughts. According to the Laboratory of Neuro Imaging at the University of Southern California, the average person has 48.6 thoughts per minute.[11]

The fears

Many men's lives are shaped by an ongoing fear of rejection, being judged by others or not fitting in. They're afraid to fail and equally afraid to succeed. Constantly feeling judged, they are afraid of being seen for who they really are – they are worried that people will see through the charade and realise they are different.

My clients often say things like, 'What if my success was a fluke?'; 'What if my time has passed?'; 'I've got less ahead of me than I have behind me'; 'I'm trying my best and still feel like I'm failing'; 'I don't feel in control of my life'. These reveal the ongoing fears we just looked at. All of these fears are standing in the way of them moving from aware to awake and keeping them trapped in their own dissatisfying lives. They're making their fear into a mantra, one that's being supported by society.

Culturally, we've been conditioned to avoid failure at all costs. Too many men frame failure as defeat, which stops them from taking action or chances. The result is that many middle-aged men develop a tendency to sit on the sidelines of their life and slowly slip into accepting 'midlife mediocrity'.

Rational lies

Many men are *aware* that they're unhappy and making choices based on fear instead of hope. That's where rational lies come in: they support the fear and give it a real-life context. Rational lies happen when our brains try to make sense of a bullshit excuse, for example: 'I can't go to the gym because I have to be at work early' or 'This piece of work really can't wait, I need to do it right now'.

Resistance to our inner voice telling us something is wrong is fear-based, but hides behind rationalisation to save us from feeling the self-induced shame of living incongruently. Resistance and rationalisation go hand and hand. They're sidekicks. You might recognise some of the things we often tell ourselves to keep us going through the messiness of middle age: 'It could be worse. You'll be fine. Chin up. Things will work out.' These are more rational lies – learn to recognise them for what they are so that you can dismantle them next time you experience them and progress your life.

The implications

Allowing ourselves to be controlled by the opinions of others or our fear of criticism is, in many respects, crippling and trapping us. Men who stay stuck do so because they are fearful of letting go of what they know, but the only way forward is to push through fear. What got you here won't get you there.

When you are following what you have been told is a winning formula (stress, struggle, sacrifice = success), it can feel impossible to change. Don't pretend you can't identify with this version of masculinity. How much longer will you go on pursuing success at the expense of your relationships, ability to be physically and emotionally present and your own wellbeing?

Despite it being on the other side of fear, change is exactly what we all need. The next level of our lives always requires the next level of ourselves.

To help my clients achieve change in purpose-driven and sustainable ways, I teach them the BetterMen methodologies that we will look at in more detail in Part 3. By understanding these and the other learnings in this book, you can create a richer, more rewarding and fulfilling life.

The men who work with me are able to create deeper connections, have high energy, experience a clear and calm mind and feel an intrinsic sense of personal purpose. They unlock how to use their strength for service, not status, and that starts with alignment.

FINDING ALIGNMENT

Alignment within yourself is the core of living a purposeful, meaningful life with good mental health. Think about it: if you're saying one thing ('I value my family') but doing another (spending all your time in the office), you're out of alignment and lacking congruence. You're living a life that is not true to yourself, your own core values or your beliefs.

It's unavoidably simple: if what you're thinking isn't what you're doing physically, you won't feel how you want. Furthermore, your mind and body will tell you this. It'll start off as a whisper that you'll likely ignore, so your mind and body will then shout a little louder. This feels like anxiety, sleepless nights and racing thoughts. If you repeatedly ignore these signs, your mind and body will start screaming, which can lead to burnout, incessant thoughts and a feeling of helplessness or frustration. Panic attacks sit waiting at the extreme end.

You need to bring yourself back into alignment to improve your sense of self and life. I truly believe that for many professionally successful men, poor mental health is caused by them being out of alignment. I've watched as my clients have faced their fears and created alignment. From there, they have been able to recalibrate themselves, redefine their lives and create a state of healthy mental wellbeing.

If you know you need to get the hell out of no man's land, you've got to do something about it. I am not suggesting you throw in the towel or quit your job; instead, I am asking you to consider leaving behind what no longer serves you.

No more success without fulfilment. It's time to realign your life by losing your mind and coming to your senses. Are you ready? In the next chapter, we'll journey onwards and see how the crossroads of masculinity mirror the choices you'll face in your own life.

REFLECTION EXERCISES

- How would you describe your work/life balance? How would the people closest to you describe your relationship with work?

- What is your definition of professional success? Are you able to articulate it succinctly?

- Open your mind. Other than money, what else would you say makes a man's life 'rich'?

- Having read what you've read, what do you recognise you're sacrificing for your need for success?

- Which three anti-values reflect the life you're currently living most strongly and what are the consequences of living life from these values?

- Look back at 'perceived' past failures. Which ones have taught you your biggest lessons? What did they teach you?

5

The Choice

You're standing at a crossroads when it comes to the journey of your life. Now you have a choice to make, one that you were probably previously unaware of because no one ever teaches this in school or society. It's the choice between going back to the old blueprint or moving forward with the BetterMen blueprint.

The old blueprint represents the system set up by men for men that is no longer serving us. Leaving this behind means moving past our fear and breaking away from the traditional and outdated constructs of masculinity. This is not an easy choice. Changing our life requires rethinking our mindset; it also takes courage.

What happens if you can't decide? If you don't decide which blueprint to live your life from, life will simply decide for you. You'll plod along with the default old blueprint.

By this point in the book, you're likely realising that you hold the power to change your life. The choice you now face may not be easy, but it is simple – to choose a better blueprint for you or let life dictate your future. Let's say that you choose the BetterMen blueprint and recognise that there's no future In the past. What would that transition look like?

It'll be nothing you haven't done before. Life is a collection of transitions. We go through cycles: from studying to working; from being single to engaged to married; from no dependents to becoming a parent. My hope is that you're now transitioning from being aware to awake; from being in the passenger seat to the driving seat of your life.

I was once where you are now. I stood at the crossroads and recognised that I wasn't who I wanted to be; that I wasn't living my life the way I wanted to live it. I knew beyond doubt that I needed to take a different path, so I did.

Now I've left the crossroads behind, I consider myself a conscientious objector: I refuse to follow the old blueprint of masculinity that requires me to be the strong and silent provider and focus all of my efforts on my career – at the expense of my health and happiness. By writing this book, I am working to help other men live by the BetterMen blueprint, bust through the myth of masculinity and teach our children, particularly our sons, a better, more encompassing version of masculinity. This is a decision that each and every one of my clients has made. They deliberately took responsibility for their experience of life – and 100% of them are glad that they did.

This chapter is designed to help you understand this critical choice and steer you towards the blueprint that creates both a professionally successful and thoroughly fulfilling personal life. My vision is that from the positive consequences of my work – the coaching, courses, social-media content, podcasts and books – the men of our era will rethink and redefine the standards of what it means to be a successful man, moving away from material possessions and cash in the bank towards personal pride, happiness and self-worth.

CHOOSE YOUR BLUEPRINT

Many men feel uncertain when they find themselves standing on the precipice of a big life change like this. It's strange. You'd think that living in unhappiness would motivate them to run towards a better blueprint with open arms, but the problem is, they are living in a state of Stockholm syndrome.

This term is used to describe a psychological state in which people who are taken prisoner or hostage develop positive feelings towards their captors over time. That's exactly the case for modern men. Caught in the societal game of life, the rat race and social-media submissiveness, we've developed a psychological bond with our captor – the old blueprint of masculinity.

Combine this with the fact that our natural trajectory is the path of least resistance, it makes sense that we find comfort in what we've always done. We are surrounded by a false sense of safety, given to us by the patriarchy. We think that playing the game of life will bring us happiness, but in reality, it is a system of control that has nothing to do with happiness. I say we need to forge our own paths.

Why the old blueprint is flawed

Let's look at the old blueprint of masculine success. In this flawed blueprint, we achieve professional success as a priority. On top of that, we build wealth and assets. The next building block is our relationship with our partner and family, our friends and colleagues, who are vitally important, but can still create their own unique pressures.

Finally, sketched in last in the blueprint, furthest away from the foundations... we prioritise ourselves. Does it seem healthy always to leave ourselves last? Of course not.

Many men, including myself before my midlife breakthrough, are guilty of putting everything and everybody before themselves. I propose there should be a new blueprint – the BetterMen blueprint. This is my solution; it's what I create the space for men to achieve when they work with me and recalibrate their own lives.

The BetterMen blueprint

In the BetterMen blueprint, we value, connect and commit ourselves to ourselves. We're clear on who we are and how we will live; awareness, discipline and effort are our allies.

Next, we focus our time, effort and energies on our key relationships. We're present with the people who enrich our lives and thus deepen our connections. If we have them, we nurture and support our children, and we align ourselves with growth friends – the ones we will continually want to deepen our relationships with. Then, we use our financial position to create greater life experiences and build the kind of memories we'll never forget, the ones that give us purpose. Finally, the last building block is our continued professional success. This is the new winning formula for men who are professionally successful or on the path to achieving this.

When you've done the hard yards, you've made the sacrifices, doing more of the same can and will prove costly. If work continues to get the best of you and your life and family get what's left of you, you may have all the trappings of success, but you certainly won't feel like a success.

Author David Brooks talks about the two mountains of a man's life.[1] The first mountain represents striving for success, recognition and power. The second represents seeking happiness, health and fulfilment. Men that stay stuck in the old blueprint can feel like they're completing repetitions of the first mountain their whole life. That sounds pretty exhausting, doesn't it?

The old blueprint of masculine success

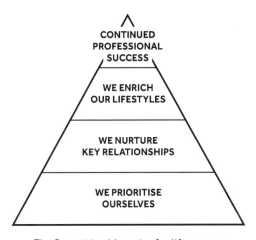

The BetterMen blueprint for life success

A choice for an era

You aren't alone in this choice. All of modern masculinity is there with you. The reality is, it's unfortunately become socially acceptable for successful men to be unhappy, and to hide it behind fake smiles and unproductive busyness.

When I say what I am about to say, I mean it – it's up to us to ensure we don't pass the old blueprint on to the next generation. Children don't learn from what we say; they learn from our example. I believe we're on the cusp of a real change, so let's give them a better example to learn from.

Society tells us our happiness comes from getting what we want. When we get what we want and we're still not happy, we've been taught and conditioned to push harder, completing more repetitions of the first mountain. We believe that we just haven't done it 'right' yet. The next generation sees us stuck in this continuous struggle, trapped in our own lives by our work, expectations and definition of success.

We need to stop living life from the anti-values. Let's let go of the old blueprint, break free from our false comfort and create the capacity to move on.

A nod to the new-man blueprint

What kind of men can we model ourselves after? Turn on the TV and you'll see that aspects of modern-day masculinity are already changing, but look a little closer and you'll likely realise that things aren't changing in the direction we want. There's a 'new-man blueprint' out there, but the truth is that it falls flat.

Generally speaking, new men are seen as nice, soft and sensitive. They're a counterculture to the strong, silent version of masculinity, but this is not rooted in real purpose or meaning.

The old blueprint told us to protect and provide, prove our self-worth through work and continue this until retirement. But going along to get along is self-betrayal. Is that it, then? A binary choice between the old blueprint and the new-man blueprint? No – as we have already discussed, there's a third blueprint to choose.

The BetterMen blueprint proposes that we should prioritise ourselves, be self-aware (a prerequisite for any change), have a sense of deliberate purpose (an assertive energy about us) and be emotionally expressive (know how to regulate our emotions and articulate how we're feeling). Change starts with us. Men, are you seeing the choice becoming clear? Will you be early adopters?

PROMISES OF LIFE

The countless self-help books, podcasts and documentaries available to us nowadays show that there is a real thirst for knowledge. Men want to know how to live well, how to make their lives matter.

As a stepping-off point, one principle men have rallied around on their path forward is Stoicism. In this context, I am talking about the ancient Greek school of philosophy that taught its followers to live wisely in harmony with nature and that virtue is based on knowledge. Unfortunately, I find that men typically confuse it with the modern-day noun; they think Stoicism means being shut down and emotionless. They emulate this and find themselves stuck, full of what I call 'misplaced Stoic resilience'. Unhappy in life (again), they think they're being Stoics by pushing on through, but in reality, they're just being too stubborn to stop. This intensifies their negative experience.

The reality of Stoicism is much more about wisdom than shutting down. We'll go into this subject more deeply in Chapter 8, but for now, I'll share the four Stoic virtues: wisdom, justice, courage and moderation. Achieving these comes from a place much more considered and thoughtful than misplaced Stoic resilience.

Moving towards the BetterMen blueprint means bearing in mind a few important factors, some of which are perfectly captured by author Richard Rohr in his book, *Adam's Return*.[2] Rohr developed what he calls his 'promises of life' to show us that in building complex societies and adhering to sophisticated societal rules, we can easily lose sight of life's basic facts. These basic facts enable us to keep life in context and make better, more informed decisions.

The promises of life are:

1. Life is hard
2. You are going to die
3. You are not in control
4. Your life is not about you
5. You are not that important

Consider those learnings. Some may be quite confronting when you see them written out like this, but the truth is, life is short and the end is inevitable. A false sense of control; the idea that everyone is judging and watching us; the comfort of thinking we can leave things until tomorrow – are all symptoms of the patriarchal structures that keep us bound and confined in our narrow definition of what it means to be a man. These ideas will stop us from living a happy and fulfilled life.

Richard Rohr's promises, on the other hand, will put things into perspective and hopefully inspire change. If you keep going how you've always gone, you'll end up where you've always been, and what a waste that would be. As boxer and activist Muhammed Ali so rightly said, 'The man who views the world at 50 the same as he did at 20 has wasted 30 years of his life.'

How should you view the world and live your life? With the courage to follow your own answers and live in alignment with your true values. You don't need a life quake for that; you can make a conscious decision to get started today simply by defining your vision of the life that you want to lead: after all, vision drives decision. You can work and live the way you want, you can change the system and live from the BetterMen blueprint so that life works for you instead of against you.

THE HERO'S JOURNEY

Making life work for you takes courage, but it's an adventure we've all seen play out in front of us. TV, films and fiction books follow this hero's journey; *Star Wars*, *Lord of the Rings*, *Rocky* are all based on the premise of a protagonist, often an unlikely hero, who goes on an adventure, faces a crisis, overcomes a challenge, and returns home transformed in some way.

Joseph Campbell, an American writer and professor of literature, described this hero's journey as the monomyth.[3] He used this to deconstruct and compare teaching within religions. One of his key findings was that a foundational element of the hero's journey is leaving the known and travelling forth into the unknown – something you are now gearing up to do.

Taking inspiration from the monomyth, let's examine what this will look like.

The call to adventure: you'll receive a life challenge inviting you to become a better version of yourself.

Crossing the threshold: you'll step over the line, demonstrating a high degree of commitment to the challenge and, potentially, change.

Being tested: your character and resolve will be tested significantly. As a result, you'll be forced to rise to the occasion.

The return: having overcome life's challenge, you'll arrive back where you started, but feeling innately different and powerfully transformed.

Like the hero in movies, we never really know who we are until we're tested to and beyond our perceived limits. Albert Einstein once said, 'Adversity introduces a man to himself'. Men who accept the call to adventure grow as a result of the adversity they experience. Men who refuse life's call stay stuck at the crossroads.

Unlike in movies, the consequences of your journey are real. Life's destination is death, so it's important to do it right. Having been on this journey myself, I'll tell you that it's not an easy one, but the sense of ownership you get from taking back control of your life is empowering beyond measure.

Your attitude towards your choice

When you're faced with the choice to change your life, you need a healthy balance between realism – 'Yes, this feels a bit shit right now' – and optimism – 'I know things can, and will, get better.' As Austrian psychologist and philosopher Viktor Frankl put it, 'When we are no longer able to change a situation, we are challenged to change ourselves.'

Nothing is more relevant for describing the attitude you need at the crossroads than the Stockdale Paradox.[4] Admiral James Stockdale was a United States Navy Airforce pilot awarded the Medal of Honour in the Vietnam War, during which he was captured and held prisoner in what was referred to as the 'Hanoi Hilton'. He survived repeated and regular torture and impossible living conditions for over seven years.

When he made it home, he said, 'You must never confuse faith that you will prevail in the end – which you can never afford to lose – with the discipline to confront the most brutal facts of your current reality, whatever they might be.' Essentially, he was saying you have to hope for the best while being realistic about the worst. Your mindset is your key strength here, which must translate into action. Blind optimism with no action may be tempting, but will get you nowhere.

That's exactly your current situation at the crossroads, so take this mentality and apply it to your own life journey. At the end of the day, the only choice you have to make is between the short-term pain of change vs the long-term discomfort of staying the same. Think about that. You may be confused and uncertain, but that's where Stockdale's optimism comes in. You have to own the facts of your reality, lean into the fear and extend your comfort zone to complete your hero's journey.

LOW SELF-ESTEEM

It's important to take the time for some self-reflection. Consider who you really are right now and who you intend to become in your future. I believe men today have a lack of personal awareness driven by a lack of cognitive bandwidth and because the 'bliss' of ignorance is easier than the discomfort of their reality. But all real change starts with self-reflection, and an ideal place to begin here is by examining your levels of self-esteem.

Self-esteem is a multi-faceted, complex picture built up by every past experience you've ever encountered. Succinctly put, self-esteem is your opinion of yourself. It's how you feel about your qualities, attributes, abilities and limitations. Having healthy self-esteem means feeling good about yourself most days and seeing yourself as someone who deserves the respect and consideration of other people. Low self-esteem, on the other hand, means that you see little value in who you are and what you bring to the table.

Men who have high levels of self-esteem play to win in the game of life; men with lower levels play not to lose. Low self-esteem can be crushing. Impacting your perception of who you are at a fundamental level, it can negatively affect your relationships, your career and your health in a variety of ways.

The way you were raised, the conditioning you experienced and the habits you have formed can and will influence your self-esteem. Self-worth, self-confidence and self-belief are all self-generated on a continuous basis. This means you have the power to switch 'off' automated processes in your brain that lead to low self-esteem, and switch 'on' thoughts and feelings that will engage and empower you. You just need to understand how.

Imposter syndrome

Have you ever felt like you're not as competent or qualified as people think you are? That you're somehow tricking them, hiding behind a mask, faking it? That's imposter syndrome. This has links to being a perfectionist and the feeling comes from something inside of you believing you aren't doing things 'perfectly'.

For context, imposter syndrome often shows up in the form of self-doubt, be it in work, intellectual intelligence or personal achievement.

Inner critic

When you try new things or assess a situation you've just handled, is the voice in your head calm and kind, or negative and critical? If it's the latter, your inner critic has taken control and is impacting the way that you perceive everything. Instead of celebrating your wins, you're focusing on all the things you've supposedly done wrong.

Usually without us knowing, our self-talk creates our mental state and the ever-present voice within is what guides our trajectory and shapes our reality. Guess what: we don't need to listen to our inner critic. It's a thought pattern and we have the power to switch it off.

Self-sabotage

When your self-esteem is low, you may find yourself engaging in destructive behaviour aimed at yourself. You may not notice it at first, but it comes in the form of negative thinking patterns and habits, disorganisation and indecisiveness that can undermine your efforts and stop you from being where you want to be in life. Examples of these destructive behaviours are: leaving everything to the last possible minute; over or under eating; avoiding reality by bingeing on social media, alcohol or porn; or simply chronic tardiness. Think of self-sabotage as a mild form of self-harm.

Shame

Shame is destructive and a major symptom of low self-esteem. For many men, the reason they stay stuck in life is because they harbour a subtle sense of embarrassment and shame. Thought-leading author Brené Brown defines shame as the sense that there's something fundamentally wrong with me and I am unworthy.[5] She goes on to point out that when we feel ashamed of ourselves, we're afraid of being different, of not fitting in, so we hide in corners and stay 'safe', never taking risks. This comes from a normal evolutionary place – we all want to belong, but when we tell ourselves that we don't, our levels of self-esteem get worse.

All of this happens inside our heads. All of our beliefs, even the ones we secretly harbour, carry with them consequences. We have the power to improve how we think, but to do this, we need to understand the ways that low self-esteem influences our psychological reactions to the world:

- **Compulsively controlling.** We raise the bar of success to unreachable heights for ourselves and the people around us, putting immense pressure on both ourselves and others. It's impossible to achieve healthy self-esteem when we constantly see ourselves as failing our own high standards. This ties in with being a perfectionist and self-defeatist martyring tendencies.

- **Victimhood.** Do you believe that you have control over the outcomes you experience? If not, you might fall into victimhood and unknowingly disempower yourself. Scientists in a recent study say 'Victimization becomes a central part of the individual's identity.'[6] They experience an external locus of control, meaning they feel completely out of control of their own life's outcomes.

Do either of these reactions resonate for you? Remember, your life moves in the direction of your strongest thoughts. Wherever you arrive in life, your thoughts have taken you there. The power lies completely within your mind and there are only two types of thinking: reflecting and ruminating. Reflective thinking is conscious consideration of past experience to enable progression, whereas ruminating is following the same thoughts around and around, creating a state of stagnation and low self-esteem.

Reflection vs rumination

The main reason men ruminate is that they are not practised in interpreting their feelings to make considered decisions. By developing self-reflection skills, we let go of ruminating and develop better emotional intelligence.

So, how do we get out of our own way and dismantle the blockers in our path? Through creating a mindset shift, promoting better self-esteem and enhancing our emotional intelligence. This means moving away from excuses, realising that every 'reason' we have told ourselves for not doing what we need to do is just an excuse.

Your new mindset requires you to consciously move on from excuses and get out of your own way. This may feel uncomfortable and you may want to hold on to your old way of being, but remember, in most cases, what you're trying to hold on to wasn't really working for you in the first place. Take the time to focus on yourself and what does work for you.

IMPROVING YOUR SELF-ESTEEM

Improving your self-esteem and self-talk is a journey. It's one that I'm intimately familiar with.

In 2017, in the midst of my identity crisis, before I recalibrated my life, I was spending Christmas Day alone, separated from my family. After drinking bottle after bottle of wine, far from sober, I opened a book that I had been gifted by a friend (which I originally had no intention of reading as I knew it had a spiritual bias).

The book was *Untethered Soul* by author Michael Singer.[7] I turned the pages and, within a few short chapters, had learned that I didn't have to listen to my inner critic; the one constantly chastising me, reinforcing my fears and relentlessly reminding me of my failings in every facet of my past. I learned how to calm my incessant mind and dilute my future fears. The mental fog that had clouded my judgement for months started to lift.

Next, I began recalibrating my life by leading myself consciously, effectively and in alignment with who I wanted to become. These actions laid the foundations for the purpose-driven man with high levels of self-esteem that I am today.

As you move forward from the crossroads towards recalibrating your life, you'll see how your own progression perpetuates positive changes in your self-esteem. In a way, your self-esteem changing is part of your hero's journey.

These are some key elements of improving your self-esteem:

- Knowing your own strengths and weaknesses and accepting them without critical judgement.

- Understanding your personal narrative – recognising your past doesn't need to imprison you in the present.

- Recognising and handling fear – you can't be afraid or anxious of the future because it doesn't exist yet.

- Conscious change – you may have dedicated your life to putting on a show, but now, you need to turn that energy inwards and cultivate change.

- Focusing on your positive achievements and accomplishments, regardless of size or significance, to forge your new, more purposeful identity.

To change your experience, you need to change your narrative. Everything you want but don't have is out of your comfort zone; now it's time to go and get it. That is your path forward from the crossroads.

Getting out of your own way

You're faced with the choice between the old blueprint and the BetterMen blueprint. The details of your progression may be unclear; they may evoke a sense of anxiousness, but perhaps now you see life choices you never knew existed. What do you need to do to take that first step into the unknown? You need to get out of your own way.

First, understand that there's only 100% of anything. About 10% of you is what you know, this comes from past life experience. About 20% is what you don't know, this is just beyond you, but it's what you are willing to explore. The other 70%? This is what you don't know that you don't know – and that's what unlocks your experience of life.

Men become aware on their hero's journey of the vast expanse of what they don't know – and that tends to scare them. When they feel discomfort, if they choose to step back to the false safety of what they already know, the result is they stay stuck.

Many men try to achieve freedom through control. They value rigidity, not flexibility. This is flawed thinking. Think about what happens when pressure is applied to something rigid. It breaks. As I've illustrated through countless statistics and studies, many men are at breaking point. They are viewing life with a rigid lens, but the reality is that the world, and the path to happiness, requires them to be flexible.

How do you avoid this process and get out of your own way? I am encouraging you to raise the bar on your own self-awareness. Be flexible and work on yourself.

The path forward

Maya Angelou, American civil rights activist, said, 'Do the best you can until you know better. Then when you know better, do better.' How right she was. You're reading this book, which is taking you to the next level of yourself – you're learning to 'know better'. The next step on your journey means translating your insights into action so you can 'do better' and live better.

Using the BetterMen blueprint, you will fundamentally change and grow as you start on the uncertain but undeniably rewarding path ahead. You will learn to let change change you, and from that, you will become purpose-driven and deeply connected with both yourself and those who mean the most to you.

When they make this choice, many of my clients report leaving behind the feeling of disconnection from themselves and creating more self-awareness than they knew was possible. If you continue with this book and join me and many other men in rethinking masculinity, you're on your way to doing the same.

One of the most important lessons I want to impart is that the only constant in life is change. Are you ready to choose your change? Chapter 6 will teach you how to take your first steps away from the crossroads to a better, more purposeful path; one that models a healthier version of masculinity than the old blueprint. One you can be proud to pass on to the next generation.

This means recalibrating your life, cultivating self-trust and activating your brain in a way that unlocks your true capacity. Let's go ahead and get started.

REFLECTION EXERCISES

- Consider all aspects of your life. What metaphorical cans are you kicking down the road? What are you continuing to do that hasn't served you in the past and what's the cost of doing so?

- If you lived life from the BetterMen blueprint and prioritised yourself more, what positive outcomes would you expect to experience?

- Consider Richard Rohr's life promises. Which one do you need to remember most and why?

- Typically, men don't consider their relationship with themselves, but if you were to describe how your relationship with yourself feels, what would you say?

- In the 'Low self-esteem' section, I shared four commonalities that adversely impact levels of self-esteem: imposter syndrome, the inner critic, self-sabotage and shame. Which one impacts you most and what tends to trigger it?

- If you had to write your own instructions on how to get out of your own way in no more than three succinct points, what would you write?

6

Recalibrating Our Lives

If recalibrating our lives was easy, we would all have done it years ago. The issue is that moving forward from the crossroads to recalibrate means dismantling years of conditioning and mental roadblocks that have developed the core of who we are today.

This chapter is all about understanding your thoughts and feelings – how they work with and against each other to create your current experience of life. From there, you'll be able to recalibrate your entire existence, shifting your perspective and living with purpose. Consider this chapter of the book your way of fixing what's misaligned.

Where are you mentally and emotionally right now? Perhaps you'll find that at this point, you're like a driver with one foot on the accelerator (your thoughts), knowing you want to make changes in your life, and one foot on the brake (your emotions), being worried about the 'how'. It seems like a lot is happening in your head, but in reality, you're going nowhere. There's a storm of thought and feeling all around you and you're stuck in the centre of it.

If you're reading this book, I'm guessing you're on the upward curve in your career or running a successful business. Your thoughts and feelings may lie in conflict at this point as your position creates a constant undercurrent of pressure and tension which can hold you back from achieving a happier life. Many of my clients experience the side effects of success that we explored in Chapter 1: never being able to switch off or relax; a lack of time for relationships; constant stress. Their career journey up through the corporate ranks or starting a business meant following a clear path, but when they finally rise to high-level seniority, they discover a far greater weight of expectation and pressure on their shoulders than they anticipated.

This creates an incessant anxiousness. They're constantly looking backwards, checking who else is climbing their ladder or studying their profit and loss statement. Every decision they make feels weighty and has a high level of consequence.

When I was in a senior military role, I was told the old adage that with great power comes great responsibility. That struck me as a profound statement and has never left me. You need to consider how you deal with responsibility. When you have reached professional success – from the point of view of the old blueprint, at least – you can make the mistake of treating everything so seriously that you create and reinforce your own stagnation. Then, you slip into a harmful mindset of treating life like it's a task without end, ticking the boxes of professional success without paying attention to personal wellbeing.

You can't keep treating your existence this way. Life's so much more dynamic than that. You need to learn from your errors, take risks and live boldly to consistently experience a happy, present and fulfilled life.

Having arrived at this chapter, you're likely already feeling more aware of yourself and the life you're living. Perhaps you're feeling the need to recalibrate aspects of your seemingly 'successful' life. Don't be disheartened; remember, when you know better, you can do better, and importantly, any setback makes space for a comeback. It's time to get into your mental machinery and examine your thoughts, your feelings and your relationship with yourself.

As we begin this chapter, I invite you to consider it's not 'negative' to think about the problems you are likely to face in your journey. In fact, it is foolish not to. To recalibrate and become fit for service, inside and out, you need to develop a capacity for staying true to yourself under pressure, be it mental, emotional or physical.

CULTIVATING SELF-TRUST

On this journey, nothing is more important than cultivating a strong and healthy relationship with yourself. You need to trust your intuition, trust your values and trust your internal compass.

Too often, in the old blueprint of masculinity, we have been taught to listen to the opinions and thoughts of others to guide our way, whether it's society's expectation of how we should live our lives or tracking cookies targeting us with what 'they' want us to buy. Those things have become our reality, but here's the truth: someone else's expectation of us doesn't need to be our reality. In fact, it can't – not anymore.

In this chapter, we will dive into how to create and lead your own vision of yourself. That work starts here and now with cultivating more trust in yourself.

You may not trust yourself right now. That's OK, but why don't you have a sense of trust in yourself? Because your brain has been conditioned to compare, be critical and self-conscious. Then the outdated blueprint of masculinity adds another layer – you find that you don't keep your word to yourself by doing the things you said you would do.

Think about it. You may have told yourself you'd join a circuit class and get fit, but that gets overtaken by work. You may have recognised a need to spend more time with your partner, but that too gets overtaken by work. Then you tell yourself that this is OK because you're just doing what you need to do to provide for your family.

You may recognise this thought pattern as something we looked at in Chapter 4 – rational lies, the excuses we make to rationalise our unhappiness and our unhealthy choices. At the end of it all, we rationalise why our entire lives have gone off course.

The reality is, we're setting ourselves up to fail and sowing the seeds of distrust within ourselves. As American physicist Richard Feynman said, 'The first principle is that you must not fool yourself and you are the easiest person to fool.' Would you trust someone you know to be a liar? Probably not, but by now you're likely to be recognising you've being deceiving yourself.

There's another way to live, guided by your own intuition and internal compass. Doing so unlocks a whole world of happiness. As poet and philosopher Johann Wolfgang von Goethe wisely put it, 'As soon as you trust yourself, you will know how to live.'

Learning to cultivate trust in yourself is one of the main things you need to do to transform your life. How do you go about doing this? I advise my clients to follow the principles below for a life in alignment where the foundation is self-trust:

- Raise your levels of awareness
- Manage your inner critic
- Live with greater intentionality
- Value and keep your word
- Get out of and stay out of your own way

We've covered various elements of these principles throughout the book, but we'll continue diving into them in this chapter. Following these principles and recalibrating your life with a better foundation of self-trust starts with gaining more capacity.

GAINING MORE CAPACITY

Recalibrating your life may seem hard, but hard issues don't always have to have hard answers – instead, what they do require are well thought-out resolutions. A main resolution in the BetterMen blueprint is creating more capacity for yourself.

Capacity. It's the one thing we all need – more space between our thoughts and in our diaries. At the moment, your life may be zooming by on autopilot, with little space to think or feel. If this is the case, your thoughts will be continuously playing out over and over again. You'll be worrying about this and overthinking that.

This needs to stop. How are you meant to make informed choices in all that chaos? You need capacity to reflect, develop and grow.

I teach my clients to make space between their thoughts so they can create cognitive bandwidth. Cognitive bandwidth enables them to problem solve, direct their focus and resist impulses. With more capacity and greater cognitive bandwidth, my clients relearn how to understand and interpret their feelings and let those feelings guide them – this is the internal compass.

Then, we translate that to their physical world. My clients learn to diarise and implement uninterrupted distraction-free time in their lives. No more automatically saying yes to work commitments with no boundaries. No more putting off the things that matter to them, like family time. One of the key methods we use is called pattern interrupt.

Pattern interrupt

Busy pattern-driven minds happen because we're trying to solve a problem we don't understand. Unfortunately for us, we live inside a problem that is impossible to fully understand: modern life and the old blueprint of masculinity. We learn to cope with life inside the problem by getting busy with work, but this is just a coping mechanism. Coping mechanisms that may have worked in the past won't necessarily support us in the future.

The thing with thinking patterns is they are pretty easy to interrupt – when you know how. Just one spanner in the works and they are completely thrown off track. Have you ever interrupted someone's story at a dinner party to ask a question and realised that you've broken their train of thought? They can't remember where they were in the story and the flow is gone. This is an example of interrupting their thinking pattern.

Pattern interrupt is a concept from neuro-linguistic programming. To get more capacity in your thoughts, you need to leverage the fact that your brain works in this way. The idea, as applied to the BetterMen blueprint, is that your brain is running on autopilot, feeding you a pattern of unhelpful and hindering thoughts. These patterns rush by, pulling you into spirals of negativity and self-doubt that can last for hours, days – and even years.

You have to break the pattern. When you notice yourself following a frantic pathway towards worry and self-doubt, command 'STOP!' in your mind. I am a believer that complexity opposes action and that's why this simple tool is so effective.

Over time, stopping the pattern becomes the new pattern. You break the chains of the autopilot thinking and free up mental capacity for self-reflection. This helps you to look objectively at your thoughts, and then implement the space and time you need to do the things you love, whether that's sports, hobbies or spending time with loved ones.

This has proven incredibly effective for my clients, giving them a new lease of life. Without capacity, days repeat. Every day is like Groundhog Day. Life is dull, void of contrast. Gaining more capacity (both mentally and physically, in terms of time) gives people the ability to bring joy and liberty back into their lives.

Changing perspective

Greater capacity will help you to gain and, if necessary, change perspective. Perspective is a commonly used phrase, but do we really understand it? It's so much more important than many people think; it's the lens through which we view our own reality, and how we view our own reality dictates the meaning we give to what we're experiencing.

Unless we look at life with a high degree of objectivity, we can easily get sucked in and carried away. Many men find their perspective clouded by society's herd mentality – this is how we get bogged down, feeling heavy with the weight of our own feelings of stress and frustration. To change this, we need to change ourselves. We need to stop focusing on the symptoms: the locked-out calendar; the flippant spending; the feelings of disconnection, and instead focus on the root cause. The root cause is almost always perspective.

You and your perspective are part of every problem you experience. Though it may not sound like it, that's good news because it means you're also part of every solution that you can apply to your life. The control is entirely in your own hands. All it takes is a little perspective shift to translate that into new behaviour.

Jack Canfield, a pioneer of personal development, said, '...every outcome you experience in life (whether it's success or failure, wealth or poverty, wellness or illness, intimacy or estrangement, joy or frustration) is the result of how you have responded to an earlier event in your life.'[1] His formula goes like this:

Event + Reaction = Outcome

The way you perceive anything you encounter will inform your reaction and therefore dictate the outcome you create and experience. With more capacity and a better perspective, you will react in ways that align with how you want to be and how you want to live. This in turn will impact the outcomes you experience. If you want to change the results you get in the future, you must change how you respond to events you encounter today.

Remember, the space between how you feel and what you do is governed by your emotional maturity. It's time to interrupt your thoughts to really think. Emotional maturity already plays an important role in your life; it enables you to gather some control over your feelings – you're not going to throw your drink at the TV screen every time your team misses a goal because you have the emotional maturity to reflect and consider your feelings before you translate them into action. You need to build on that and apply it to the more complex situations in your life.

I'm not saying this will be easy. You're up against quite a few obstacles and the first is your brain itself. The reason why you may find yourself with a negative perspective, dwelling on mistakes or fixating on critical feedback, is because negative events have been found to have a greater impact on the brain than positive ones. This is called the negativity bias.[2]

As humans, we register and record negative events in a far stronger and more impactful way than positive ones. This causes us to remember adverse experiences more vividly than good ones, to recall insults more readily than praise and make decisions based on negative information instead of positive.

You have the power to hack this natural brain setup by engaging in positive self-talk, reframing situations and establishing new patterns. Whether your mental cup is half full or half empty, with the correct skills, your cup is refillable.

HOW TO SHIFT YOUR PERSPECTIVE

All real change to your life requires a shift in perspective. This won't be a one-off thing; you need to change the lens through which you view your entire life. If you briefly lose perspective, moving forward, you need to know how to regain it, but it'll be worth it. Paraphrasing the words of author Dr Wayne Dyer, 'when you change the way you look at things, the things you look at change', including yourself and your life.

It's time to dive in and examine the mechanisms that drive your behaviour and day-to-day choices. We'll do this by looking at the think-feel-do-be loop.

We operate in a subconscious loop that creates who we become. This loop starts with thinking, which impacts our feelings. Our feelings in turn drive the things we do and don't do, and what we do over time determines who we become. This would all be fine if the 'thinking' step was always logical and true to our values, but the reality is, it's not.

Biologically speaking, we are adaptability machines, but our brain, our software, favours efficiency and pattern thinking. In other words, it favours the path of least resistance, so it thinks, acts and reacts in the same ways, defaulting to autopilot.

It's true. The vast majority of our behaviour is rooted in subconscious pattern thinking and autopilot.

We need to exercise greater control over what and how we think. Thoughts and feelings are like a two-way feedback loop, creating an echo chamber that influences our behaviour and who we really are, building our reality.

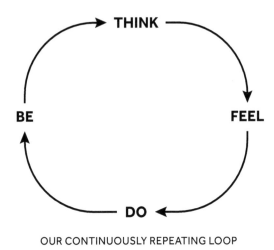

OUR CONTINUOUSLY REPEATING LOOP

The think-feel-do-be loop

Learning how to think

In school and life, we were never taught how to think critically or with emotional maturity. Learning how to think is a skill and a discipline. It involves a mixture of evaluating our automatic assumptions, tuning into and understanding our feelings, and tempering those with our expectations and goals. The Cherokee legend concerning an elderly brave who tells his grandson about life expresses this well.[3]

'Son,' the brave says, 'within all of us there is a battle between two wolves. One is evil. He is anger, envy, jealousy, sorrow, regret, greed, arrogance, self-pity, guilt, resentment, inferiority, lies, false pride, superiority and ego. The other wolf is good. He is joy, peace, love, hope, serenity, humility, kindness, benevolence, empathy, generosity, truth, compassion and faith.

'The same fight is going on inside of you and inside every other person, too.'

The grandson thought about it for a minute, and then asked his grandfather, 'Which wolf will win?'

'The one you feed,' he replied.

Take a moment to consider which wolf you've been feeding in your life. Learning how to think means learning to feed the positive thoughts – the ones that build your character and are aligned with your values. To do that, you need space (in BetterMen terminology, that's capacity) to step away from the barrage of pattern thinking and consider life objectively.

I'll now walk you through my three brains theory, which many of my clients have found useful in examining and changing their own thought patterns.

THE THREE BRAINS

You may think you know where your brain is. You may think you only have one, but the truth is that you're influenced at any given time by three brains.

The head brain

This brain is like your mental dashboard. It's logical, rational and problem solving, but it can also stray into overthinking and fall victim to automatic patterns. It's actually the root cause of many modern problems, so it's not entirely to be trusted.

As we discussed in Chapter 4, the average person has 48.6 thoughts per minute.[4] That is a lot of background noise in your already-busy life. If those thoughts are running wild with no control or perspective, you might soon find yourself overwhelmed and engaging in automatic behaviours with no logical root.

Renowned neurologist Donald Hebb stated, 'Neurons that fire together, wire together.' This means that the more we think certain thoughts or engage in certain behaviours, the more the brain automatically strengthens shortcuts to those behaviours and thoughts. In terms of operational efficiency, it's amazing. In terms of quality of life, not so much. We follow old patterns and become cemented in certain habits without even realising we're doing it.

On top of this, the things we think about most are more available to us and we can access them easily. This is called the frequency illusion.[5] After noticing something for the first time, we tend to notice it more and more, making it seem that it's appearing more frequently in our lives. For example, once we decide we 'need' a new BMW, we'll start seeing that particular make and model of car everywhere.

The thinking brain is not some infallible computer. In fact, it's pretty illogical – full of shortcuts and boxes to put the world into to make it easier to comprehend. It can also go into overdrive, creating anxiety. Anxiety happens because we're addicted to knowing – we want to be certain about everything because certainty gives us security (in our minds).

The issue is, life isn't something we can take shortcuts through, and it's far too vast to put into easily understood boxes or completely control. We need to take our steer in life from something more than just this brain.

The heart brain

The heart brain is our emotional range. It's our feelings and emotions, our connection to ourselves and to others. This can massively influence our behaviour, but we often get it wrong by failing to correctly interpret our emotions. Instead, we react automatically and forget to make space to breathe and really listen to what our feelings are telling us. In the moment, we don't choose how to feel; instead, how we feel is an innate response to what we're experiencing.

Emotion is much harder to measure and objectively define than other areas of social science, but according to new research, there are twenty-seven different categories of emotion which all interplay and blend with one another to form a much more sophisticated range than we may believe.[6] However, people usually just focus on their basic six emotions: happiness, sadness, fear, anger, surprise and disgust.

Along with previous generations of men, we've been taught to disconnect from our emotions, but in reality, this detaches us from ourselves. We need to spend less time in our heads and more time interpreting our feelings and listening to what our emotions are telling us. Why? Because everything feels better when we do – believe me (and my hundreds of clients).

Listening to the heart brain and redirecting the energy of the head brain is one of the main things you can do to shift perspective and recalibrate your life, but it's not the only thing. Another key player is the gut brain.

The gut brain

The gut brain is the oldest brain. It goes by many names – intuition, inner voice, sixth sense. Whatever you call it, it's usually subconscious and it's usually right. After years of conditioning, though, we make the mistake of not trusting or discounting our intuition. This needs to change.

I'd encourage you to give up thinking and listen to this older and wiser measure of the world that we all carry within us. Intuitively, in most situations, we know what to do and when to do it. In studies, participants relying on intuition alone made the right call up to 90% of the time when presented with split-second mock stock-market decisions.[7]

Because of how much we overthink nowadays, we lose the skill of gut thinking in our day-to-day lives. We're the only animals that think about their thinking, and now we've lost our instinct.

To recalibrate your life, you need to create the capacity that enables you to listen to your gut brain in conjunction with your heart brain. The powerful combination of intuition and feeling can help you to make clear, congruent, value-driven decisions about the direction of your life. Once you do, you'll see and feel your life changing right in front of you.

Applying this to your life

Remember, we don't experience life; we experience our thoughts. I can't stress this enough. Thought has the power to be either creative or destructive, and our thinking will create either personal freedom or personal imprisonment. As we've seen, we need to listen to the heart brain and the gut brain more in unison. Awareness of our selves is the gateway to ongoing positive change: the more questions we ask, the more we learn; the more we learn, the more we ask. It becomes a self-perpetuating cycle of personal learning and growth.

THE FOUR PILLARS OF PROGRESSION

The purpose of this chapter so far has been to help you work through the elements of your life that will lead to recalibration and alignment. Alignment is a core concept here: your thoughts, feelings and actions need to be working together. In other words, how you think has to translate into physical action. The think-feel-do-be loop must be congruous and work harmoniously if you're to create and live a life you enjoy.

You may now be wondering how you actually implement these changes. The four pillars of progression provide a structure for you to use to implement lasting change.

Awareness

This is the first pillar. We have to become aware of our experiences, and do so without judging them or what we find. This helps us to pinpoint what may be misaligned or out of sync between our thoughts and our behaviour. As psychologist Carl Jung stated, 'Until you make the unconscious conscious, it will direct your life and you will call it fate.'

The opposite of awareness in this context is **autopilot**. This is how you may have been living up until this point. This has to stop, today.

Acceptance

When we become aware, we may find things that are uncomfortable and have to face up to some hard truths. Acceptance means not falling into victimhood or blaming others, as this is disempowering and shifts our control of our self to others. Essentially, we need to think about the things we're doing while we're doing them and find alignment within that, accepting that what we're experiencing is ours to own.

In this context, the opposite of acceptance is **avoidance**. It's shifting blame to others and living in a state of victimhood.

Action

Living with a bias towards action is a guiding pillar: it means that after becoming aware of what we need to do, we do it. Hopefully, our action is derived from the heart brain or the gut brain and we've taken the space to really process it before doing it. Action is the difference between trying and doing. A lot of men try, but few do.

In this context, the opposite of action is **passiveness** – our lives are defined by passiveness when we follow the old blueprint of masculinity without ever looking up or questioning why.

Accountability

Maintaining accountability is the final guiding pillar. We have internal accountability (keeping our word) and external accountability (inviting someone to help keep us accountable) and both are equally important.

Accountability means taking responsibility, following through on what we say we'll do and being reliable. It means moving away from being disengaged on autopilot.

In this context, the opposite of accountability is **irresponsibility** and overall, the opposite of progression is regression. Utilising the four pillars of progression ensures you get off autopilot, you don't avoid what needs to be done, you give up being passive and you stop being irresponsible in how you're using the finite time you have here.

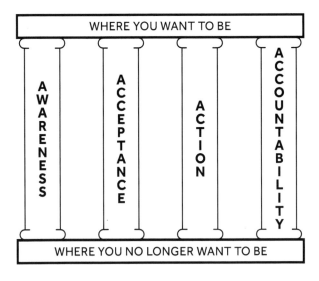

The four pillars of progression

MOVING FORWARD

In this chapter, you have encountered some key methods for recalibrating your life. Take a moment to step back and consider the journey you are on and how you will use these recalibration tools.

I like to think of recalibration as the physical journey of a farmer planting crops for the season. They first cultivate the land, then sow the seed, then nurture what they've planted. Finally, when the time's right, they harvest and reap what they've sowed. You will follow a similar process as you recalibrate your life.

Of course, this takes a mental shift. We all need to give ourselves permission to shed our old beliefs and build something true to ourselves, more purposeful and fulfilling. What keeps us stuck, unable to make that shift, is often our fear. This fear is around the judgement of others; letting go of what we've worked for; being seen for who we truly are. In other words, it's fear implanted and conditioned into us by the outdated blueprint of masculinity.

We cannot live bowing down to those fears; we need to give ourselves permission to progress our lives. When we repeatedly avoid doing hard things, we run the risk of teaching ourselves that we're not capable of doing them, but this isn't true.

Given what we've covered in this chapter, you're now likely aware that wherever you are in life, your thinking has brought you here. If you change your thinking, you have the power to recalibrate and change your life. In this part of the book, we've gone through mediocrity, no man's land, and arrived at the choice that defines the second part of our lives. Now it's time to recalibrate. I am asking you to cultivate the courage to take the first step while nurturing the discipline to take the next, and then the next and the next until your life is as you wish it to be.

The majority of men out there are searching for an external solution to an internal problem, but my clients and I know the answers are already inside us. To uncover our answers, we let our innate wisdom and our feelings guide us. This is exactly what you will learn to do as you head into the third and final part of this book.

REFLECTION EXERCISES

- If you truly trusted yourself, what would be one personal and one professional change you wouldn't hesitate to make?

- Instead of adding to your life, what does your intuition tell you that you should be subtracting from instead of adding to your life?

- In E+R=O, we discuss 'reacting'. Broadly speaking, in what situations and with what types of people do you react in negative ways?

- When you read the tale of the Cherokee brave and his grandson, what did you learn about yourself? Which wolf are you feeding?

- If you listened more to your heart and gut brains, what would you hear them asking you to do?

- Having read the first two parts of this book, what do you recognise you need to accept and potentially change about your current life?

PART THREE

A BETTER MASCULINITY

7

Self-leadership

Perhaps Part 2 was a reality check for you. Perhaps you now recognise you've been following the old blueprint and living life from the anti-values, but don't worry or judge yourself. The best thing about the past is it's already over.

In Part 3 of this book, we'll be going deeper into the BetterMen blueprint and drawing out more of the methodologies I use to help my clients live better lives. We will focus on leading ourselves into alignment, setting intentions and being more assertive. Above all, we will continue to rethink the standards of what it means to be a successful man.

Have you ever started the year with good intentions, hitting the gym a few times a week? You feel refreshed, renewed and re-energised. Then slowly, life gets in the way and your progress comes to a stop as you slip back into your habitual snacking, sedentary desk-based days. By the end of February, things are back to normal. This is exactly what we will aim to avoid by implementing strong self-leadership principles.

We're not born with an instruction booklet, but if we were, I am absolutely sure the first chapter would explain the skill and discipline of self-leadership. It's a concept that isn't taught in schools or life. If you Google 'leadership', you'll get around 3.5 billion results, but if you Google 'self-leadership', you get a mere fraction of the results. This is another way in which we are taught *what* to think, but not *how* to think.

Self-leadership is about living intentionally, influencing our thoughts, feelings and actions towards achieving our own objectives. These objectives must align with our truest selves – who we really are and what we really want. Does that sound familiar? Think back to our work on finding better alignment in Chapter 6. These are the exact lessons that will help you as you become an intentional leader of yourself.

There's no leadership gene – leaders aren't born, they're made, and how you lead yourself is directly related to your potential to lead others. Those whom you lead aren't just listening to what you say, they're watching how you live and lead yourself. In this chapter, we will aim to make your life an authentic reflection of who you are.

It's not going to be easy, but effective leaders can't choose what's easy over what's right. As author and speaker John C Maxwell said, 'Leadership is influence, nothing more, nothing less.' You're going to influence everything about your life to improve your path for yourself and for those around you. Why? Because when the leader gets better, everyone benefits. The same is true for you, when you get better, your family, friends and community groups, your business and career – they all benefit.

In my work, I repeatedly reference the importance of self-leadership, a key principle of which is accountability. For context, I define accountability as your willingness to take responsibility for your life, something I believe is an essential component of achievement. As we know from Chapter 6, the opposite of accountability is irresponsibility – you can never lead yourself if you're lying to yourself about whether or not this is needed.

Now let's look at being the agents of our own change and implementing the principles of self-leadership so we (and everyone in our sphere of influence) can benefit. It's important to note that this is an in-depth chapter covering all aspects of self-leadership. If you feel like you need to read it twice, I would encourage you to do so.

THE TWO TYPES OF MEN

There are two types of men in this world: those who are passive (letting life happen) and those who are assertive (making life happen). Over time, the old blueprint has conditioned men to adopt a passive approach, particularly so in middle age.

Paradoxically, part of this approach has centred around dominance – the old blueprint encourages us to become the go-getting leader, but by following that plan without ever questioning it, we're still passively letting life happen to us. We learn to follow the blueprint and be loyal to others – but not to our true selves. Consider this: by being loyal to others in this way, we're doing ourselves a disservice and it's adversely affecting our experience of life.

To cultivate self-leadership, we cannot be afraid of being assertive and taking the steps necessary to make life happen. Let's dive a little deeper into what it means to be assertive.

Becoming assertive

Men generally have an aversion to being assertive because they think it means either arrogance or aggression. In my mind, being assertive is simply stating what you need. It's being clear about what you require or want from a given situation. In other words, putting your own self and your own needs first in a fair way.

Most men, particularly those in the messy middle, don't consider their own needs, but if you're not putting yourself first, you'll likely be putting yourself last. The collateral consequences of this are potentially damaging. Contrary to common misconceptions, making your own needs a priority in your life is not selfish, it's necessary.

Passive men usually adopt the persona of being people-pleasing, 'nice guys'. Nice guys develop subconscious personality traits that place great emphasis on doing more for others than for themselves, being likeable and liked. Paraphrasing a tweet by American author Jason Wilson, a man who walks on eggshells will eventually become so skilled at it, he won't make a sound in life.[1] Don't let this be you.

Typically, nice guys think of themselves as doing everything right. Because of this, they tend to blame others for their own experiences, often portraying themselves as 'the victim'. Nice guys enjoy fixing other people's problems while concealing their own because beneath the surface, they're desperately seeking approval and positive recognition from others. Living life as a nice guy can be an isolating and lonely experience.

Passive men need to understand that every choice carries with it a consequence and a cost. If you're in the passenger seat and letting life happen, the cost is your own vision of your future. Nobody else is going to implement that vision or create your future for you – it's up to you to make it happen.

Assertiveness and self-leadership

Becoming assertive means understanding the impact of putting yourself last and instead, consciously choosing to lead yourself. I invite you to think about how you will assert your needs, particularly as you begin the process of recalibrating your life. Think about how you will move away from simply turning up and going through the motions, and deliberately move towards showing up and living with intentionality and purpose.

When you're considering your mindset, there's another model you might find useful. I call it the line of self-leadership. Below the line, there's a victim mentality fuelled by blame, avoidance and denial. Above the line, there's a victor mentality propelled by ownership, action and responsibility. Passive men rarely cross the line from victim to victor, while assertive men live above the line, driving their lives forward.

■ OWNERSHIP

■ ACTION   **VICTOR**

■ RESPONSIBILITY

THE LINE OF
SELF-LEADERSHIP

■ BLAME

■ AVOIDANCE   **VICTIM**

■ DENIAL

The line of self-leadership

I get it, living this way can be hard, but consider the passive alternative. To emphasise my point, let's put this into context: when you're saying yes to one thing, by default, you're rejecting, saying no to – something else. For example, because of our coaching, one of my clients realised that he was always saying yes to work and, by default, was saying no to his young family. This client ended up printing this statement:

'If I'm saying yes to this, what am I saying no to?'

This now sits in a frame next to his desk. Physically seeing this message every day means he's able to recalibrate his misaligned priorities and lead himself in conscious and considered ways.

Think about how this message could apply to your own life. Instead of resorting to default and taking the path of least resistance, face up to situations and be more assertive. It's time to get out of the passenger seat and back into the driving seat of your life.

THE THREE TYPES OF INTELLIGENCE

An effective self-leader is an intelligent leader, but perhaps not in the way you're likely to assume. A man who is a true leader of himself is one who's able to tune into and leverage the different types of intelligence we all have within us.

I'll expand. When delivering courses or facilitating coaching, I share with my clients that there are three types of intelligence:

- **Intelligence quotient (IQ):** This is our intelligence as measured by the academic standard. It's our ability to reason, pick up new concepts and understand new information to find answers, make predictions and generate educated assumptions.

- **Emotional quotient (EQ):** This is the ability to understand, use and manage our own emotions in positive ways to communicate, connect, empathise, solve conflicts and cultivate beneficial relationships.

- **Pragmatic quotient (PQ):** This is the ability to use both words and thoughts as tools for problem solving and action. It's closely linked to one's ability to apply common sense and often referred to as 'street smarts'.

Which of these really matter for self-leadership and life? As children in school, we are benchmarked almost exclusively against IQ. This means that we develop a belief that it's the most important type of intelligence, so we tend to discount EQ and PQ. The reality is, EQ and PQ are more important than IQ throughout the rest of our lives, including in our professions.

Our leadership ability comes down to EQ and PQ, and outside of academia, nobody stops to question our IQ. In his book *Emotional Intelligence*,[2] author Daniel Goleman says 'At best, IQ contributes about 20% to the factors that determine life success, which leave 80% to other forces: forces grouped as emotional intelligence.' That's spot on. Emotion and pragmatism are vital aspects of living a recalibrated life with strong self-leadership.

The problem is, we have old-world brains operating in a modern world. These old-world brains have evolved to keep us alive, not happy. Listening to our feelings of unhappiness cause us discomfort. We try to avoid this discomfort at all costs, burying our heads in distractions, but when they subside, we're left with fear, anxiety and sadness. In a world filled with high-reward dopamine hits, it's so much easier to scroll, gamble, sext, shop, eat and drink than to sit down and listen purposely to our feelings. In other words, we make it hard to allow our feelings to be our guide.

Moving forward, we need to get out of our head, the IQ brain, and leverage the primitive wisdom held in our heart and gut brains to maximise our EQ and PQ. I'm inviting you (again) to tune into your feelings. Let them serve you and guide you.

THE THREE BIG IDEAS

In my work, I teach the three big ideas as a way to help my clients implement self-leadership in their lives, and now I'm going to teach them to you. These ideas are mindset, mood set and habit set. The three combined form the foundation and fabric of our lives, so if one is neglected or left unchecked, it will adversely impact the other two.

Another way to think of this is activating our head, heart and hands to work together to create a sense of alignment in our lives.

Mindset

Our mindset matters. It is a collection of beliefs, created from past thoughts and experiences, that shapes the way we feel about ourselves and how we interpret the world. As such, it's a key factor in both our self-esteem and our mental health.

Generally speaking, there are two types of mindset: growth and fixed.

- Men with **growth mindsets** value effort and learning and believe that if they persist, then they can improve.

- Men with **fixed mindsets** believe their abilities are fixed, so they often won't try anything new because they think they'll fail.

A healthy mindset is a growth mindset. This puts you in the driving seat of your own life. It involves 'showing up' consistently in the world with persistent positivity and an open and curious attitude towards learning and developing. A growth mindset is a core element of self-leadership and stewardship of your own life.

Together, the myth of masculinity and the old blueprint actively discourage the creation of healthy growth mindsets. Instead, they promote blinkered fixed mindsets, but the truth is, your mind is malleable and re-trainable regardless of age or stage.

Neuroplasticity refers to 'the brain's ability to modify, change, and adapt both structure and function throughout life and in response to experience'.[3] Because of neuroplasticity, you can improve your mindset and rewire your brain. Personally, the main mindset change I needed to make when recalibrating was to stop taking life so seriously – being serious removed the fun for me, so I needed to retrain my brain to default back to a positive mindset. I had to learn not to focus so much on external attainment and validation. Nowadays, I believe in imperfect action and not comparing my current performance to that of others, instead comparing it to my own past performance.

Mood set

Your mood set is a transient state of being that is informed by the feelings you experience throughout a period of time. Most men are reluctant to feel their feelings (because they've never been taught how to or they believe it's weak to do so), but if they're living life in a way that doesn't make them feel good, over time, they can create a mood that traps them in their head.

When you know how, you have the power to change your mood as you see fit. Your mind doesn't know the difference between fact and fiction; it's all narrative and it's playing out every minute of every day, so by exercising control over your perception of events, you can influence and change your mood.

Think about times when you've had a bad day. Usually, this is made up of minor inconveniences: getting stuck in traffic; a meeting not going the way you planned; your inbox filling up. You know from the think-feel-do-be loop that how you feel dictates what you feel, and this dictates what you do. You can tap into that same knowledge to let feelings that don't serve you pass, and then consciously choose to recalibrate your mood to live life in a more aligned way.

Over time, this mood-set hack will enable you to rewire and create new strong neural pathways that help you to develop a more resilient and positive attitude. Viktor Frankl said, 'Everything can be taken from a man but one thing: the last of the human freedoms – to choose one's attitude in any given set of circumstances' and this is something that many of my clients find to be a useful guide as they develop a more resilient and positive mindset.

Habit set

Simply put, habits are small decisions we make and actions we take every day that build up to become our lives. Aristotle said, 'We are what we repeatedly do.' What we repeatedly do (ie how we think, how we manage our mood and how we act) over time forms the person we become because we start to run almost entirely on autopilot.

Research suggests that around 40% of our physical actions happen habitually, without conscious thought or deliberate action, and as I highlighted in Chapter 6, our brains favour pattern thinking.[4] We need to get off autopilot and back into living our lives with engagement and intention. When we learn how to transform our habits, we can easily transform our lives.

As we'll discuss later, the actions that we do and don't take shape our lives, so why can it be so hard to choose helpful habits? We're often caught in a neurotic paradox. This happens when we know not to do something – we know it's unhelpful, unhealthy or destructive – but still do it anyway. All these little self-failures are examples of poor self-leadership that reduce our ability to trust ourselves and add to a larger failure of ourselves and our life's goals.

I know from personal and professional experience that the fastest way to success is to replace bad habits with good habits. I am now asking you to intentionally decide your habits and thus decide your future.

ENVIRONMENT DICTATES PERFORMANCE AND STATE

Another important aspect for a man looking to cultivate strong self-leadership is an understanding of how our environment dictates our performance. We're constantly and simultaneously exposed to two types of environment: our mental environment, what's happening inside our mind, and our physical environment, what's happening in the world around us. To the unaware man, the two blend together to create 'his' state and inform his mood.

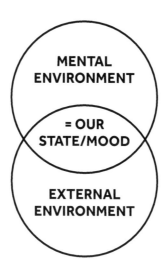

How our environments create our state and mood

We often overlook the fact that our environment can and will impact how we think. Let's examine the animal kingdom for a poignant example. 'Happiness' is obviously a human concept, which we'll explore in Chapter 8, but it can be measured in animals by health, activity, inquisitiveness and even immune-system response. Studies show that animals in captivity, when compared with animals in the wild, have lower reproductive capability and higher stress levels, meaning they are less happy and healthy.[5] Their physical environment impacts their mental and emotional state.

This shouldn't come as a surprise – we often hear that we're a product of our environment. Dr Joe Dispenza, an internationally renowned author, describes how experience and environment can shape who we are as a person.[6] First, an experience (within an environment) creates an emotional reaction. The reaction turns into a mood, which turns into a temperament, and then a personality trait. Scientifically speaking, feelings only last ninety seconds,[7] but when we attach meaning to what we are feeling, we create our mood and in turn the state of our reality.

If that's true, then we must take responsibility for the environment we create. When we looked at Jack Canfield's Event + Reaction = Outcome formula, we discussed controlling our reaction, which is closely linked to the creation of our state and environment. Leading ourselves means understanding that our environment and our reaction to it will shape who we are as a person.

THE THREE TYPES OF ENERGY

Energy is life and the energy we bring to our lives and the world around us is crucial. There are three types of energy to consider here: mental, emotional and physical. Our energy matters across these three areas.

Why is this so important? 'The world belongs to the energetic,' as American poet and lecturer Ralph Waldo Emerson said. A study claims that 70% of all communication is non-verbal.[8] This means that our energy informs people who we are and what we're about before we even begin to speak. Our energy drives and dictates the actions we do and don't take in our lives.

A by-product of the old blueprint is low energy; after all, it is hard to feel energised when we're diluting ourselves and our authentic aspirations to 'fit in'. Low energy means low levels of life performance.

A key cause of low energy and low performance is the concept of 'mental pebbles'. Our mind is full of the small things that are seemingly insignificant to us, but matter to us anyway. Because we have so many mental pebbles in our minds all the time, life can feel complex and stressful. Mental pebbles reduce our bandwidth and our mental energy.

High energy, on the other hand, enables us to execute our ambitions and achieve sustainably high levels of life performance. Our energy is our responsibility. To live a life we enjoy, it is important we make a concerted effort to raise our energy.

Let's unpack each type of energy as it relates to our lives.

Mental energy

This is the energy of our mind. It's our mental bandwidth, which translates to our ability to be present as well as our ability to problem solve.

To increase your mental energy, look at what may be holding you back or what you may be resisting in your life. See what you can remove. When you address what you've been resisting, you'll create more cognitive bandwidth and 'head space'.

Emotional energy

This is the energy of our mood and emotional state – it's fulfilment, happiness, engagement and connection. This, as we just learned, can be impacted by our environment and experiences.

Increasing your emotional energy is a matter of understanding your feelings. From there, it is implementing changes to raise your mood energy. An effective way to achieve this is by doing some form of exercise or activity outside in nature. This boosts your all-important hormones like dopamine and serotonin.

Physical energy

This is our habitual physical energy. It means feeling assured in our own physical readiness to take on the challenges of life. Increasing our physical energy is incredibly important in our modern lives.

Take a look at your physical energy right now. It's likely impacted by a sedentary desk-based lifestyle.[9] This needs to change. 'Sitting is more dangerous than smoking, kills more people than HIV and is more treacherous than parachuting,' says James Levine, Professor of

Medicine at the Mayo Clinic.[10] Far from making you feel more tired, regular exercise, even if it's just a walk around the block, is essential to maintaining high levels of physical energy. This is why many smart watches come with a tool to remind you to move every hour. If you have it, leverage your wearable technology; move, stand up, flex your arms and stretch your legs.

To reduce your mental pebbles and shift to higher levels of overall energy, you need to be present, let go of what no longer serves you and separate the things you can control from those you cannot. As Muhammad Ali, American boxer and activist, said, 'It isn't the mountains ahead to climb that wears you out, it's the pebble in your shoe.' Understanding the interplay of these three types of energy and your mental pebbles will help you to develop healthy and proactive self-leadership traits.

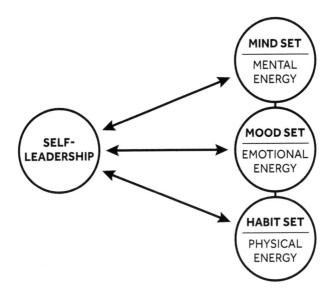

The relationship between the three big ideas and the three types of energy

YOUR APPROACH TO SELF-LEADERSHIP

Years of being trusted to support men in recalibrating their seemingly successful lives have enabled me to get clear on the core components that promote effective self-leadership. While there are many, the three I'm sharing here are those that can't be neglected.

Clarity

Clarity in your vision – in who you are and what you want – is absolutely key to strong self-leadership. Vague goals lead to vague results, so if you're unsure what you want, it's highly likely you'll fall victim to numbing out and convenient trivial attractions. Netflix's CEO, Reed Hastings, recently stated that Netflix's No. 1 competitor is sleep.[11] Without clarity, a man can easily sleepwalk through life, burying his consciousness in convenient technology and connected devices.

A man intent on living his life to its fullest potential will know what he wants and have high-level clarity about how he will achieve it. Clarity enables him to see what is distracting him from living that life – you can't call something a distraction unless you know what it's distracting you from. Beyond this, clarity translates into motivation. When my clients turn corners, they no longer need perseverance or grit if they have clarity and enjoy what they're doing.

In our modern one-click world, rife with a consumer culture, almost everything is accessible immediately, so perhaps we shouldn't be surprised that many men don't know what they want anymore. The question is, how do you create clarity in your own life? The surest and simplest way is to think critically about what you really want. Doing so will enable you to eliminate options that mean less to you and, as life flexes, realign your values to who you are and who you want to become.

Purpose

I open this section with a quote from author Alex Rogers: 'Purpose is the great divider that separates those who are simply living from those who are truly alive.'[12] Think about that. Purpose separates the two types of men we looked at earlier – those letting life happen and those making life happen – and it starts with intention. The flow of your energy, action and outcomes will go in the direction of your intention. Intentionality means re-minding yourself, which helps you to remember what's truly important in your life.

Be clear about what matters to you and who you want to be; don't let life distract you. Make that your purpose. To help me do this in my own life, I frequently use my mind's eye to create a clear image of my future self. This gives me perspective, helping me to choose aligned actions to become that ideal version of my future self.

Additionally, a useful strategy for leading yourself with less distraction and greater purpose is to front-load your priorities. This means getting to the things that matter most early in the day and early in your week. It sounds simple, but it will serve you.

I urge you, as an aspiring leader of yourself, to have intentions about what you want to do. This will help you define how you want to live.

Discipline

Discipline is closely linked to integrity; together, they're about choosing courage over comfort, despite the risk of potentially uncomfortable consequences. Together, they are vital for a life in which you lead yourself with purpose and clarity.

As I've highlighted, the world is full of distractions. It's become all too easy to live without self-discipline, but it's costlier than you may think. A life with discipline, guiding you to your own clear purposeful intentions, avoids this. As entrepreneur and author Jim Rohn said,

'Discipline weighs ounces while regret weighs tons.' It's not too late to ensure that when you're old and grey, your conscience is carrying ounces instead of tons.

It's important to note that resilience underpins each of these components. You can have clarity, purpose and discipline, but if you fall at the first hurdle, it's all for nothing.

'Resilience' is a term that has been distorted, whether it's by society or social media. People make an assumption that being resilient means not stopping, when in reality it's about regaining a state of balance or equilibrium. Resilience is key if you're going to continue developing on your journey. It has been shown to improve top athletes' mental wellbeing, self-esteem, motivation and determination,[13] and the same applies for you.

You'll find yourself presented with situations where you won't know what to do or it'll be hard to do what's right, but living a disciplined and resilient life will help you to take immediate action and maintain your momentum.

Clarity, purpose and discipline will serve you and remind you that the time is always right to do what is right.

STRUCTURE AND SYSTEMS

Nobody's perfect. No matter how aligned, disciplined, recalibrated you are, you'll still make mistakes. You'll experience good days and bad days and days where you just don't know what to do. You can't avoid that, but what you can do is plan for it.

Structure is the answer. When your willpower wanes (and it will), it's important to have a structured approach to your days and weeks to keep you in alignment.

Spending eleven years in the military, eight in the Army and three attached to the Royal Marines, I saw the power of harnessing structure and systems first hand. When I initially moved across to working alongside commando forces, I was met by a bout of imposter syndrome. Was I good enough? Would I get found out? It left me feeling a sense of trepidation.

Then, when it came to actually working with them, I was underwhelmed at first. I asked myself, 'Are these the elite soldiers that I had in my mind?' As time went on, what became apparent was that they never got bored of the basics. Their ability to lead themselves and practise high levels of personal discipline made them a world-renowned fighting force. Bottom line: we can all learn something from the Royal Marines and their ever-present self-leadership.

I'm asking you to develop tangible anchors in your day to keep you aligned. Anchors such as exercise, reading, learning, personal development, time alone or quality time with loved ones. Create daily No-Fail Goals like taking a lunch break, setting strict sleep time and making sure you move or exercise. This will keep you in the driver's seat of your life.

You may think you already have this kind of structure to your days with a to-do list, but to-do lists are often just a series of irrelevant tasks that keep you busy but won't move things forward. What I am suggesting here, through No-Fail Goals, is real structure – it creates a strong foundation for productivity and the possibility for massive action.

Tony Robbins differentiates between passive action and massive action.[14] Passive action is reading books, taking courses and talking about our plans without actually following up on them, whereas massive action is actually going out and utilising what we've learned. Are you a passive or massive action taker?

You can win back time in your diary and purpose in your life, particularly if you're feeling lost or demotivated, simply by having a structure and following it. A concept that lends itself well to better self-leadership is to Plan Tomorrow Today. You can increase your productivity by spending a few minutes planning out your tomorrow and noting down your key objectives before you do them. This simple practice invites you to utilise the four pillars of progression – awareness, acceptance, action and accountability – by living day to day with clear intent.

YOU ARE IN THE ARENA OF LIFE

You're the main player and protagonist in the arena of your life. US president Theodore Roosevelt once said, 'It is not the critic who counts; not the man who points out how the strong man stumbles, or where the doer of deeds might have done them better. The credit belongs to the man who is actually in the arena, whose face is marred by dust and sweat and blood.' That's you right now. You are in the arena of life and your choices here matter. Collectively, they inform your ability to lead yourself or fail yourself.

Choosing to stay stuck, bound by habit and routine, doesn't prevent failure; it guarantees it. You can't keep papering over the cracks. You need to create real change and lead yourself out of Dante's forest and into your new life.

To stop trying to live up to societal success and instead live a life you enjoy, really feel how it feels to be you. Raise your awareness of your current life and its trajectory, trust your intuition, cultivate a bias towards action and lead yourself in alignment.

We'll progress these ideas and learn more concepts throughout Chapter 8, looking at what opposes and what creates happiness. We'll examine our relationship with failure and why seeking work/life balance is a mistake. Ultimately, through questioning our own mortality, we'll remember life isn't a rehearsal, so let's treat it as what it is: an opportunity to live, lead and legacy build.

REFLECTION EXERCISES

- Consider your leadership. What type of leader are you? Would you want to be led by you?

- No one else other than you is 'keeping score' on how you live, but if someone was, what criteria would you want them to score you against?

- Consider the three big ideas: Mind, Mood and Habit set. On a scale of 1 to 10, 1 being low, 10 being high, what score would you give each of yours and why?

- If purpose truly is the divider between those that are 'simply living and those that are truly alive', what's your purpose?*

- Your energy communicates non-verbally who you are. In day-to-day life, what does your energy communicate to others about you?

- A key component of self-leadership is discipline. What areas of your life, from food consumption to phone usage, do you feel need a more disciplined approach from you?

* Your purpose can be anything you want. I've had clients decide their purpose is to be more present with their loved ones, to experience less overwhelm or simply to smile more.

8

Life Isn't A Rehearsal

We get one life. Just one. Questioning your mortality is one of the key themes you've likely been confronted with on your journey through this book.

The old blueprint of masculinity doesn't care about the quality of the life you live; it simply requires that you commit yourself to the daily 'grind' for an unfair proportion of your seventy-nine laps around the sun. Your mortality isn't a big consideration for a system that ships you off to an unsatisfying retirement with a high risk of dying soon afterwards and the sadly all-too-common regret that you should have worked less and played more.

The old blueprint of masculinity teaches you to treat life like a task with no end, filling your time with work and playing by somebody else's rules. This means that you're probably living a life by default instead of design.

Life isn't a rehearsal. We've got to stop treating it like it is, because a life not lived is a life wasted. Please don't waste any more of your one opportunity on Earth.

Where do you begin? You can't change the past, but you can change your relationship with it. Doing so unlocks the present and creates your future. You can choose to make the correct choice and go through a reinvention, transforming from mediocrity to meaning. You can change everything, building and living a life you no longer yearn to escape. No more drowning your consciousness in social media, news apps, work and holidays. No more days wasted in a blur of stressful firefighting. The consequences of your choice will either be imprisonment in a life described by American essayist, David Henry Thoreau as, 'the mass of men lead lives of quiet desperation', or set yourself free from what might already feel quietly desperate.

The only things we leave this world with are our memories and regrets. We're about to make sure that your memories outweigh your regrets. In this chapter, we will go through the key elements of your life that you need to examine from the perspective of your mortality.

TIME

Entrepreneur and author Jim Rohn said, 'Time is our most valuable asset, yet we tend to waste it, kill it and spend it rather than invest it.' You need to invest your time in what matters because time isn't money. Time is life. It's a finite resource. How we spend our time is how we spend our days, and how we spend our days is how we spend our decades. How we spend our decades ultimately determines whether our life was worth living, so create a healthy relationship between your time and yourself.

Let's start by looking at the practicalities. Our diaries are the gatekeepers of our time and offer an accurate reflection of our current life priorities. If someone looked at your diary right now, what would they believe your priorities to be? I'd imagine they might think work, work, work.

That's the issue. The people and things that shout loudest in life will always be the ones who demand your time, but they never tend to be your partner, your children, your friends. The things you truly enjoy and value, get pushed into the background of your life as your family and friends understand you're 'always' busy because they've been bought up in the old blueprint of masculinity too. They respect your wish to make work a priority, but this leaves you with too much time devoted to the office and too little to enjoy moments with the people you love. Moving forward, your diary needs to reflect your priorities.

When I recalibrated my life, I stopped saying to myself and others that I didn't have the time. I realised that how I spend my time is a reflection of who I am and who I am choosing to become. Time is always available and how we spend it really does reflect our priorities.

I decided to prioritise myself and my family. Will you?

FAILURE

You've almost certainly heard people say, 'Failure is not an option'. It's usually quoted in a social-media meme, but it accurately reflects a core social teaching plucked straight from the old blueprint of masculinity.

We have it ingrained in us that we need to avoid failure at all costs, so we struggle with it whenever it happens to us. From school to the boardroom, failure feels wrong, painful, challenging to accept, but the truth is, if we struggle with failure, we'll struggle to live a truly successful purpose-driven life. Failure is a natural part of our human experience – if we're living meaningfully beyond our comfort zone, we'll encounter failure regularly.

I am encouraging you to respond to failure positively, which starts with your perspective. How you view failure will impact how you live your life. The way you respond to it determines everything you experience, so consider failure in a new way.

What if failure wasn't losing? What if it were only feedback? Seeing it as a learning opportunity, a chance to try again with more information, can really alter your outlook and your life.

The BetterMen blueprint approach to failure involves keeping the learning opportunity and life lesson it gives front and centre of our experience. The way that BetterMen clients and I see it, failure is natural and normal. It happens, we expect it and we build upon it. Failure is a comma, not a full stop. As author Robert Kiyosaki states, 'To face your failures and learn from them are at the core of success.'

If we give ourselves permission to shift our perspective on it, failure becomes a natural part of the process from which we develop and grow as men. It really is true that good times don't shape us, tough times do. For me, reaching rock bottom was far more educational than any of my successes. You could say I failed my way to purpose. As author Stephen McCranie tells us, 'The master has failed more times than the beginner has even tried.'

Let's look at failure from another angle. Ray Dalio, leader of Bridgewater, the oldest hedge fund in the world, states in his outstanding book *Principles*:[1]

Pain + Reflection = Progress

He explains that our most painful moments are often the most important ones; the ones that create the reflective insights that afford us true progression.

To truly progress, we need to consider the words of musician Frank Zappa: 'Without deviation from the norm, progress is not possible.' For too long, men have been cowed into a herd mentality caused by the old blueprint. Yes, deviating from this herd mentality means venturing out of your comfort zone, exploring new horizons and learning to fail well, but it's 100% worth it.

While you're reflecting to progress, there are a few common pitfalls to watch out for. Many men will use their problems to re-affirm their thinking. They'll go round and round in circles, living life below the line of self-leadership, becoming victims, and that will keep them trapped.

Tell me, who and where do you want to be in the future? To answer this question, you need to look forward, but you also need to reflect on your own perceived failures. Taking this a step further, you can look back and examine your entire life through this reflective lens.

YOUR STRATEGY FOR LIFE

Ironically but perhaps unsurprisingly, most professional men will have a business plan or a career progression plan – even if it's written on the back of a napkin. They may even have a plan for their next year of holidays, but in almost all cases, they won't have a family plan or life plan.

What's your strategy for life? Most likely, you don't have one. Like most men, you can all too easily fall into the trap of not planning; of thinking that a strategy for life or family isn't necessary. Knowing that life isn't a rehearsal and that you need to prioritise and plan the things that matter to you should change that thinking.

Your approach today

Modern men's life approach is not guided by strategy. As Canadian psychologist Jordan Peterson puts it, 'Random wandering will not move you forward; it will instead disappoint and frustrate you and make you anxious, unhappy, and hard to get along with.' Most modern men simply plan for quantity. They frantically squeeze as much in as possible, when really they should be focusing on quality, but that's the harder plan. It takes more courage.

In his book *Good to Great*,[2] business strategist Jim Collins states that having more than three priorities means you really don't have any. Remember this whenever you're tempted by the easier 'planning for quantity' route.

How can you create and change your life strategy? It starts with developing a clear image of your future self: who you will become and what you intend to achieve. This creates perspective and a direction to align yourself to. Without this, you don't give yourself permission to enjoy what you've accomplished. Your finish line of 'life success' is always moving and enough never is enough. You're back to living life in the rat race, suffering with the anti-climax of achievement.

Everyone's strategy for life will be different. A personal rule of mine that keeps me true to my life's strategy is that if I am considering an important life choice and I can't decide, the answer is no. This stops the indecision, procrastination and worry and provides a foundation to move forward from. Knowing what you don't want can be more empowering than knowing what you do. Take a moment to consider that.

The ladder of first-world life

Let's look at our first-world lifestyle from a broader perspective. Imagine there's a 'life ladder' and we're all occupying a rung. At the bottom of the ladder is survival, at the top significance. The higher up the ladder you are, the better your life and the more you've used your time here on Earth to achieve and experience.

I'll break the rungs down. Read them like you'd climb a ladder, bottom to top:

Significance (legacy building). You feel proud of who you are, the life you're living and your legacy.

Sustainable success (consistent happiness). It feels good to be you. You're consistently happy.

Success (fulfilling). Your achievements matter; you feel a subtle sense of fulfilment.

Striving (demanding). You can sense your progression; life's engaging, but demanding.

Struggle (firefighting). Your experience of life is a constant battle; you're always firefighting.

Survival (tiring). You feel reactive and emotive and live a stressful and tiring life.

The ladder of first-world life

What rung of life are you on? How long have you been there? Adapting the words of Professor Leon C Megginson, it is not the strongest of the species that achieves significance, nor the most intellectually intelligent; it's the one who is most aware and adaptable to change.[3] Aim for significance at the top of the ladder. The path there isn't always easy and you will feel out of your depth at some points, but use your adaptability to change. It's all too easy to get stuck at the bottom of that ladder.

Many men achieve professional success in the first half of their lives and stay stuck there. There's a country mile between a subtle sense of success and being proud of who you are, the life you're living and the legacy you're building. What got you here – the rung of the ladder you're on currently – won't get you there – the next rung up.

You won't achieve significance by chance. To achieve significance, you need to think about your approach and be unafraid to deviate from your expected pathway.

This change of approach starts with thinking about your relationship with other people. Do you want to impress or impact people? If you're looking to impress them, the chances are you'll stay stuck between survival and striving, always trying to prove your worth on the bottom half of the ladder. If you focus your strategy on adding your unique value and creating an impact, then you'll consistently live your life in the top half, between success and significance.

HAPPINESS OVER SUCCESS

The average man isn't happy. The average man, in fact, rates his happiness at just 6.3 out of 10.[4] This is because we're stuck in the myth of masculinity with a fixed mindset and an incorrect understanding of success. We've been sold the wrong idea of what true success is – more and better of everything than the Joneses – and we've been measuring our self-worth against the wrong yardstick – our net worth.

Money is never a good motivation for success. It creates a situation where the more successful we become, the more pressure we experience, the more we have to lose and the more hours we need to work to stay afloat. Money should simply be seen as our way to create unique experiences and powerful memories.

Happiness is a mindset

We spoke about fixed and growth mindsets in Chapter 7. It's relevant here, too. Success can be suffocating for those with a fixed mindset. After all, how do we achieve more if we believe our abilities are fixed? We need to shift to a growth mindset, which means that we believe our skills and successes are flexible and adaptable.

With a fixed mindset, we think our happiness comes from getting what we want, and when we get what we want and we're still not happy, we've been taught and conditioned to push harder and work more. A growth mindset, on the other hand, creates a flexible path to personal happiness built around applied effort, personal persistence and an intrinsic desire to improve. A man who functions as an effective leader of his own life understands that growth is constant.

Happiness is something we need to shift our focus towards as part of our broad life strategy. If we do, I am convinced there will be less of the five challenges I discussed in Chapter 1: workaholism/burnout, loneliness, poor mental health, midlife crisis and divorce. All of these are born from the myth of masculinity that keeps men chasing a flawed and fake definition of success.

Navigating towards your own happiness

Until you're happy, you won't appreciate your own success. As a leader of yourself, you have a responsibility to defend your happiness (which I would suggest is a better measure of success than material possessions in the second half of a man's life). As German theologian Albert Schweitzer said, 'Success is not the key to happiness. Happiness is the key to success.'

What do you do that you enjoy? What makes you come alive and feel fulfilled? Opposing this – your happiness – are often the things you tell yourself you want, because wanting something is a contract you make with yourself to be unhappy until you get it. Learn to align your 'wants' with your priorities, time, effort and energy, and centre all of those around your happiness. You'll soon see results.

Consider this: navigating towards happiness means doing more of what you love, less of what you tolerate and none of what you hate. Learn from the top five regrets of the dying. Don't be the old man lying in his bed, wishing he'd been true to himself and lived a more purpose-driven life instead of being chained to his desk.

I'll share a personal experience on this. A client recently asked me how I would define success. My response was 'Consistently experiencing health, happiness and liberty'. To make that tangible, I went on to share my intention to implement my definition of success by achieving a net figure in my business while working a three-day week. This is me making my vision of life success my reality. What's your definition of success and can you articulate how you will achieve it?

Buoyancy, not balance

Imagine a set of traditional weighing scales, perfectly balanced, holding equal amounts at the same time. We've been led to believe we can achieve this perfect balance between our work and our life. I say this concept is a lie.

Why? It's practically impossible to have work and life equally balanced at the same time. It implies you can give 100% at work and 100% at home, all within the same day or week. Research by Stanford University shows that this is not the case.[5] In fact, the participants who multitasked performed worse on memory tasks than those who did not. As productivity consultant David Allen said, 'You can do anything but you can't do everything', especially not at the same time.[6]

Let go of the idea of balance. Abandoning balance was a huge catalyst for my sense of purpose and fulfilment. Instead of balance, I adopted buoyancy.

Buoyancy is best understood by considering a concept I call the sea of life. When the tide of your life rises, be it caused by work pressure, family conflict or the geopolitical situation, being buoyant keeps you on the surface and prevents you from drowning in busyness. It will enable you to stay afloat with visibility of the world around you so you can proactively make informed and aligned choices as opposed to reactionary fight-or-flight decisions.

What creates the ability to be buoyant? We're back to capacity. The chain anchoring a buoy to the sea bed of life allows it to rise and fall with the tide. As men, we need this sort of capacity. The more capacity we create, the less stress, frustration and tension we will experience, and the most effective way of creating capacity in our busy lives is to build in boundaries.

BOUNDARIES

Boundaries are the limits we create to protect ourselves from a world filled with the wants and needs of others. They guard our time, space, energy and self-esteem, giving us a clear view of ourselves in the now and the future.

A key boundary to set is around work and time. Parkinson's Law states that work expands so as to fill the time available for its completion.[7] You likely know that if you have a hard deadline, you can get a certain piece of work done in an hour. Conversely, if you don't set a hard stopping point, you'll waste time through distraction, procrastination or making minor revision after minor revision. When you're living life from the BetterMen blueprint, it's critical to have boundaries around how work impacts your life. I advocate for work-life integration, not work-life conflict, and the best way to achieve this is to set boundaries around time for yourself.

How to set boundaries

By setting boundaries, you create clarity and capacity. Without clearly communicated and upheld boundaries, frustrations build up, which can turn into resentments, which can manifest and show up as anger, either passively or overtly – both at home and in the workplace.

There are three stages to creating better boundaries:

1. **Create**. Identify what you feel you lack, and then understand what you want instead of what you've got. For example, perhaps you want more quality time with your family and to spend less time working.

2. **Communicate**. Share this to those around you. For example, to gain time back from work, you may need to delegate more to your teams, so you need to ask them to take on more responsibility.

3. **Uphold.** When your boundaries are tested – and they will be – you need to have the moral courage to back them up. For example, this may look like refraining from firefighting and fixing problems for your teams. Not only will this give them back the autonomy to solve their own problems, it will ensure you protect your family time.

Beyond boundary-setting, you'll face situations where your boundaries are pushed. In these cases, the most important word in the world is no. It's what differentiates the average man from the successful; the passive man from the assertive; the 'letting life happen' man from the 'making life happen' man. Remember, if you're going to say no, say it early. Be direct about it, don't put it off and be positive – say it expecting a reasonable and beneficial response.

PRODUCTIVITY

Conventionally, being productive refers to the efficiency with which you can complete tasks that are important to you, but leadership expert Robin Sharma's definition of productivity resonates much more with the BetterMen blueprint: 'Productivity is less about what you do with your time. And more about how you run your mind.'

Think about that. Productivity is about how well you manage your mind. A well-managed mind doesn't ruminate or procrastinate; instead, it reflects and is deliberately intentional.

At the core of productivity is intentionality. If you live with intentionality, you'll act in alignment with what you value and create a sense of meaning in your life. When I am coaching clients to become more productive, it's through the lens of 'getting shit done', which is about accomplishing and achieving what they intend to do.

The irony of being productive in the way that society defines it (working hard and producing significant output) is that others then expect more of you, not to mention you're likely to expect more of yourself too. For a man who often dips below the line of self-leadership, becoming productive by optimising his performance can actually be counterproductive – he should be vigilant for this.

Creating real productivity

Day to day, you may find you have a tendency to manage your time around the schedules of others, but to create a version of productivity that works for you, you need to stop this. A man living above the line of self-leadership will correct this imbalance and create carefully crafted boundaries so that others manage their time around him.

To achieve this, you have to have an awareness of your priorities. Think about your priorities and categorise them into low, medium and high. In particular, watch out for medium priorities. These are distractions – they steal your time, effort and energy. They are neither crucial nor unimportant, but they tend to be the biggest strain on your levels of productivity. Review what you currently consider medium priorities and re-categorise them where possible to either low or high; aim to have as few medium priorities as you're able.

SELF-CARE

Self-care is misunderstood by men. It is another victim of social-media memes that condescendingly tell us what we should be doing to look after ourselves, but it really can't be ignored.

Alongside setting out your boundaries to be productive, you also need them to make and protect the time to take care of yourself. It's all too easy to get sucked into a busy life, caring for clients, contracts, family members and friends without ever stepping back and reflecting on whether you're OK. You need to learn to defend your time so that you have space for self-care. You can do this by using the three-stage boundary creation plan.

Treat self-care like you would any other high-value commitment. Create capacity and space for yourself. Time blocking is a key way to achieve this. This means consciously assigning time to certain priorities or commitments, usually in one-hour blocks.

My suggestion is to schedule self-care into your calendar and treat it with the same intention you would give to any other high-value meeting or commitment. Remember, if you don't make time for your wellness, you'll be forced to make time for your illness. To use the Monopoly board as an example, it's a bit like 'do not pass go' if your self-care and wellness aren't in order.

It may feel strange, perhaps selfish to put yourself first like this, but if there's anything I've learned on this journey, it's that the best way to take great care of your family is to take great care of yourself. Self-care is the key to consistency, which we'll discuss in the next and final chapter.

The types of self-care

Self-care exists on three planes: mental, emotional and physical. I have identified these 'big four' as being the most important elements of successful self-care:

- **Sleep** is the Swiss Army knife of health. It enables you to function at consistently high levels and keeps your body and mind rested and healthy. The National Sleep Foundation guidelines suggest adults need seven to nine hours of sleep per night.[8] Anything under seven hours is classed as suboptimal.

  If you're someone who already knows the benefits of sleep in theory, but tends to suffer from insomnia, you're likely to find that if you prioritise time for self-care, this will take so much pressure from your shoulders, you'll no longer lie awake in the middle of the night with your brain racing. For those of you with anxiety-driven insomnia (and let's face it, that's usually the cause), a great book to read is *Don't Feed the Monkey Mind* by Jennifer Shannon.[9]

- **Nutrition.** You really are what you eat. Avoiding sugary, highly processed foods is common sense, but not common practice. Giving your body nourishing, healthy food is a vital form of self-care that enables you to perform at your best. Take care of your body; it is the only place you have to live in.

- **Movement.** I am an advocate of movement in any shape or form. The more you move, the better you'll feel. Going for a walk or a run or to the gym promotes better mental health and a strong, healthy body long term.

- **Connection.** Authentic, meaningful relationships are necessary for a healthy life. In Chapter 1, I mentioned the Harvard Happiness Study, which shows that those with meaningful social relationships live longer and feel less lonely, anxious and depressed than those without.

If you don't take care of and service yourself as you do with your car, you will break down. Applying the big four, with an emphasis on sleep as a foundational component of your overall health, will improve your mental, emotional and physical wellbeing.

FASHIONS CHANGE, BUT STANDARDS DON'T

You may still be asking yourself, 'How do I set myself up, in terms of my mindset, to live a life above the line of self-leadership?' To answer that, I suggest we turn to the practice of Stoicism. In ancient times, a philosopher was a lover of wisdom. Wisdom, in my mind, is turning knowledge into action, and that's where the Stoics relate to the BetterMen blueprint in the present day.

Stoicism is a school of philosophy that was developed in ancient Greece and Rome. It aims to maximise positive feelings, minimise negative ones and help you to hone your virtue of character. For me, the three Stoic maxims that have most stood the test of time are:

- **Know thyself.** This means having greater awareness of what you do and don't know, recognising both your abilities and limitations. Be acquainted with your past, but don't be bound or limited by it.

- **Nothing to excess.** This relates to not spreading yourself too thinly or overcommitting in any aspect of your life – including work. Intentionally manage your commitments and your priorities to live a happy, buoyant life.

- **Surety brings ruin.** Surety mirrors certainty; it shuts us down and disables our abilities to think, feel and learn. If Admiral James Stockdale, who we met in Chapter 5, had assumed a stance of surety during his time as a prisoner of war, he wouldn't have survived his imprisonment.

These maxims create a solid mindset guide for living a strategically aligned life. Seneca, the Stoic philosopher, said, 'It is not that we have a short time to live, but that we waste a lot of it.' Consider that. This book is about recalibrating how you live so you don't waste your life. It's about rethinking masculinity so the blueprint you pass on to future generations of men is fit for purpose. Modern-day philosopher James Pierce said, 'To be Stoic is not to be emotionless, but to remain unaffected by your emotions.' This is how I apply Stoicism in my life. When something external happens, I consciously choose not to allow it to dictate my internal, emotional state.

Mortality was a theme in Stoic life that seems to have been forgotten over the years. The Stoic phrase *memento mori* translates as 'remember that you have to die'. Ancient wisdom and philosophical tools from the Stoics can enable us to live in what they described as *'Eudaimonia'* – human flourishing. Why wouldn't we want that for ourselves?

Time and time again, professionally successful men fall into the trap of thinking they're the only ones experiencing an unhappy life. With the self-imposed pressure to succeed and constant comparison to other men, they feel it's impossible to be their true selves. They don't realise that they are not alone. It saddens me, but I believe that many men make being who they want to be the hardest thing to do in this modern life.

It doesn't have to be this way. The BetterMen blueprint calls for professionally successful men to rethink what they want to use their time for, to live life with a sense of deliberate purpose and be emotionally expressive.

If we stop letting our days pass us by, we can be the catalyst for meaningful masculine change and create a fully functioning, fit-for-purpose blueprint for the generations that will follow us. How do we actually implement this change? We need to act on what we know as opposed to what we do not, and we need to start acting now. Creating change and continuing on the path to a new and better way of living can be challenging, but it's well worth every step.

As we close this chapter, I want to leave you with my favourite quote by the Scottish philosopher Thomas Carlyle: 'Go as far as you can see; when you get there, you'll be able to see further.' Even if you're reading this book with brain fog, I am only asking you to go as far as you can see.

Consider that: you only need to go as far as you can see...

The last chapter of the book will look at the types of life you can choose to live, the BetterMen values and, most importantly, how to implement them. It will also serve as your guide in rethinking masculinity. Let's take the next steps right now.

REFLECTION EXERCISES

- Time is life. How much of your life is actually your own? What would you need to delete or delegate from your life to get more time back?

- Life isn't a rehearsal. Imagine you're a ghost at your own funeral. What do you hope to hear said about you?

- Without a strategy for life, you will falter. If someone were to ask you, 'What's your strategy for life?', what would you tell them?

- On the ladder of first-world life, what rung are you on? How long have you been here and what are you not doing that you know you need to do to get to the next rung?

- In the BetterMen blueprint, personal happiness is foundational. Think about or, better, write down at least ten things that make you happy. Read them daily.

- Now you understand the importance of boundaries, identify at least three boundaries that, if you were to uphold them, would create and increase your capacity.

9

Becoming Better

As we step into the final chapter, I want to take a moment to recognise both the journey of modern men and the journey you have been on over the course of the book.

You may have picked up this book feeling a sense of disillusionment. A feeling of fatigue. You may have been tired of living the same day over and over, dreading your mornings, battling a full inbox, shuffling through a packed diary and juggling endless commitments to both work and family. You may have felt disconnected from your partner, your family and yourself, without ever being able to put your finger on what exactly was wrong.

You are not alone in this; you are one of millions of men who have been conditioned since childhood to follow the old blueprint of masculinity that is making them unhappy, unhealthy and uncertain. This old blueprint tells men to suppress their feelings and ignore their intuition. It tells them to lead and care for their families, teams, businesses and communities without ever taking a moment to consider how they are leading or caring for themselves.

The old blueprint of masculinity is presented to each of us from birth as the 'way things are done', along with a clearly defined vision of what a 'successful man' looks like: 2.4 children, a life partner, a dog, a large house and expensive car. Men everywhere are following this default path, feeling lost as they live a life they don't understand. We've all been conditioned not to question it, not to speak up.

This vision of success – when we really examine it like we did in Chapter 1 – is damaging. It comes from our grandfathers' and fathers' generations. Post-war fathers often built simple, quiet lives for themselves, but their sons grew up wanting more. They wanted success, wealth and status symbols – a counterculture to the humble way they were raised. This has been passed down to us.

Today, men are busy overworking and under-living to achieve 'success' as it was defined in the past. In reality, this means we're busy losing time for anything meaningful or rewarding. Sometimes, success and happiness coincide, but often they oppose each other, forcing us to choose one or the other. As I've shown throughout this book, too many professionally successful men are making choices they'll likely regret.

The world around us doesn't make things any easier. Society is moving and changing more rapidly than ever. Developments in technology, politics, globalisation and more mean that we're living in a world that's unrecognisable from 100 years ago, so why are we still using a blueprint that's more than a century old? With the metaverse, cryptocurrency and artificial intelligence, life is being sped up, automated and digitised, but because of the deeply entrenched patriarchy, masculinity is moving slowly.

We are facing an immense pressure to succeed, in the traditional sense of success, in a world that is changing every day. Social media and advertising have made perfect look normal and good appear disposable. The goalposts are always moving and the prizes are always bigger, better, more.

When we're climbing the ladder of first-world life, in 'striving' for traditional success, we're living our lives asleep. The world is telling us what to think and we think it, fitting our stories, our lives into the wider societal narrative. The chapters in this book are designed to increase your awareness of modern-day masculinity and wake you up so that you can live a life you enjoy.

As we embark upon the ninth and final chapter of the book, I want you to remember not to succumb to the pressure to conform. Don't waste any more time before implementing the BetterMen blueprint in your life. You can become part of a movement of men no longer choosing to partake in the traditional game of life where they are expected to leave their homes early in the morning to jostle with the herds of other commuters, only to arrive at large glass-boxed buildings where they'll remain seated indoors for ten to twelve hours before returning to the discomfort of their home where they'll eat, scroll and watch TV until lights out. This cycle is repeated decade after decade and only defused by the occasional holiday.

There's no 'someday', only today. Grasp it. As author Paulo Coelho puts it, 'One day you will wake up and there won't be any more time to do the things you've always wanted.' The time is now. Make the choice; make the change.

The only thing that makes change hard is our own fear and resistance. Chinese philosopher Confucius said, 'Life is really simple, but we insist on making it complicated.' We're not going to overcomplicate things here. I intend to show you how to use the BetterMen methodologies to make your life sustainably enjoyable and simple. Then it's over to you to create capacity to lead yourself, to hear your own intuition and recognise what your feelings are communicating before rolling out recalibration across your life.

CAGED TO CHARGED CONTINUUM

All men live life on a continuum that ranges from caged to comfortable to charged. Many do not realise that they're stuck at one end of the continuum: caged. It doesn't have to be this way. Learning to leverage this continuum unlocks a connected and vital way of being.

- **Caged.** When you're caged, life is defined by a sense of isolation. You feel that nobody can understand how challenging your current situation is, constantly asking yourself, 'Is this it? Is this my life?' You tend to lose your temper often and live with a warped, unhappy perspective.

- **Comfortable.** Despite having your basic needs met and thinking you have everything you require to be 'happy', you quickly realise that there must be something more; something beyond the creature comforts sold to you by targeted ads.

- **Charged.** A charged life feels energising and exciting. Consider it your flow state where you're regularly 'in the zone', doing what you love and seeing tangible results. You take on challenges and you're enthused by doing so. Sensing you have presence and a deep purpose, you're active and firing on all cylinders, doing great work and creating connected relationships.

Like hundreds of my coaching clients before you, you can use the methodologies in this book to move from your caged or comfortable life to living and feeling truly charged. Charged in this context equals success and unless we feel successful, we won't reach the best phase of life: significance. It's the final stage of the journey.

Most people will take themselves from caged to comfortable, but few will create a charged life. Therefore, few will transition from success to significance. To know their life has mattered, men need to choose to live a charged life. It won't happen by default, but by intentional design.

The charged life is hard to achieve for the average man because since childhood, he's been set off course by the flawed old blueprint of masculinity. If you let it, society will continue to set your bar of success. You'll stay in the same lane, with the same standards and expectations as every other man – most of whom, as we know, are unhappy. Remember to keep choosing the charged life and pursuing personal purpose.

I want to leave this section with this concept: your greatest assets are your time, effort and energy. If you manage these poorly, you'll feel overwhelmed and frustrated and stay bouncing between caged and comfort – you'll believe that the most you can hope for is to live a comfortable life, but really, a comfortable life isn't comfortable. It's just familiar. Manage these assets well and you'll be energised and engaged. You'll live a charged life.

THE SKILL OF BEING A MAN

By now, you understand that 'being a man' and 'masculinity' are not the same thing. Being a man means being expressive, loving and caring.

A man holds within him a special set of strengths and sensitivities. We've been conditioned to cultivate our strengths and ignore our sensitivities – qualities like understanding, empathy and compassion – but if we only play from our 'strengths', we're only half as good as we're capable of being. We need to live from our strengths and harness our sensitivities. In doing so, we will develop the skill of being a professional man.

As journalist Joshua Foer said, 'The way to get better at a skill is to force yourself to practise just beyond your limits.' Fortunately for us, every day, life creates situations that are just beyond our limits, enabling us to practise the overall skill of being a man.

Let's now look at three individual skills that I have identified as the most important for being a man. These, of course, tie into the themes of alignment and rethinking masculinity:

- **The skill of thinking.** You change your life by changing your thoughts. You need to think clearly and critically and leverage your intuition. By developing the way you think – listening to your three brains – you will unquestionably become a more skilled man.

- **The skill of feeling.** Feelings tune us in to our real selves. They work like an inbuilt satnav system that helps us take the right turns at the right times in life. Practise the skill of detecting and not judging your feelings. This process will keep you in awareness.

- **The skill of doing.** This means living a defined rather than a default life. It encourages us to live less out of habit and more out of intent. It's how we turn our insights into actions and create new, more favourable outcomes.

These skills will serve you well on your path to becoming a BetterMan. Beyond these, in my work, I've developed two further skills that can help with their implementation.

Checking in

Checking in with yourself means intuitively or intentionally setting time to examine how you feel. The best way to do this is to implement a system around it.

An example of this would be asking yourself every morning, afternoon and evening, 'How am I feeling?' If you're unsure of how you feel (because the old blueprint required you to numb your feelings), I'd recommend you look up The Feeling Wheel by Dr Gloria Willcox.[1] Take a screenshot and use it as a reference point – this has helped many of my clients to develop the skill of detecting their feelings.

Consider this practice your safety net, protecting you from a downward spiral towards unwanted emotions, as well as being a springboard for experiencing more favourable emotions.

Expressiveness

The second way to cultivate the skill of being a man is expressiveness. I want to be clear here: there's a current social-media movement spread via memes about men needing to be more vulnerable, but this misses the point. Men don't really need to become vulnerable (which we often translate to feeling open to criticism, judgement or attack), but we do need to be expressive.

This can be hard. Most men have no safe space in which to share and express their feelings, but talking saves families, friendships, marriages, careers, businesses – and lives. By talking expressively, we decompress. Bottling up, on the other hand, only intensifies our experience. Instead of manning up, we need to focus on opening up.

Life experience is the hardest teacher. It tests us before teaching us the lesson, but we can learn more about ourselves by hearing the experiences of others. We can learn from one another and grow from the expressiveness of other men.

Consider the men you admire, men who have managed to become successful in business and in life, and find out what they did to get to the rung of significance on the ladder of first-world life. Whether you ask them directly, listen to their talks or read their advice, you will likely find that far from being in competition, they're happy to give back and help other men join them at the top of the ladder. They have truly mastered the skill of expressiveness.

Prevention is better than cure

You've probably heard this old adage many times, but there's wisdom in it. Once you start leading yourself, you need to prevent your life from slipping back to its previous state.

Let's walk through key areas of life and consider in advance how to stay proactively aligned in each one:

- **Relationships.** You can create and continuously improve relationships by spending quality, unrushed, uninterrupted time with those you value. As a side note, if a relationship breaks down because of your growth, I would encourage you to let it go. Do not feel bad for outgrowing people who will have had the chance to grow with you.

- **Health.** You can improve your health by prioritising self-care. To create purposeful progress in your health, remember not to judge yourself by unfair, unrealistic standards. You may not be in your physical prime anymore, but you can still find a health-focused lifestyle that works for you.

- **Work.** Despite leaving work until last in the BetterMen blueprint, I am not anti-work. Your work matters; perhaps more than you realised before turning the pages of this book. You can improve your sense of professional purpose by engaging in work that you find meaningful. You'll never get tired of work that enthuses you; that you find rewarding.

- **Happiness.** When you get off the hedonic treadmill and stop trying to buy happiness, you can increase your levels of happiness by feeding the 'right wolf' – the one that is focused on joy, kindness and compassion – and by bringing greater intentionality to your relationships, health and work.

THE BETTERMEN VALUES

If knowledge is power, this section of the book is going to empower you.

A trend I see with many clients is that men confuse their values with social ideals. A social ideal is simply what society tells us is right. It is also worth noting here that many men confuse and use virtue signalling to be seen as doing the 'right thing' in front of the 'right people'. If you do this, stop it, it corrodes your self-esteem and takes you firmly out of life alignment.

What are values? Paraphrasing the words of author and thought leader, Dr John Demartini, your values are your voids, your voids form your goals and your goals shape your life. Think about that. Your values are things you don't have and a goal is something achievable that helps you to fill that void.

To bridge our voids and feel positive about ourselves and our lives, we need to learn to live life through our values. Doing so will provide a strong sense of direction. It will make decisions less difficult, anchor emotions and keep us in integrity with ourselves. For men that are clear on their own individual values, life is simpler.

The BetterMen values are the values I feel we as men lack. Carefully collated from thousands of hours of authentic coaching conversations with men just like you, they are the voids of today's men. Coincidentally, the values that will help you 'see' your way to your goals all start with the letter C.

Let's explore the voids we need to bridge to rethink masculinity.

Courage

Courage, the first BetterMen value, is a catalyst for action. Without it, fear dominates both our decisions and actions. Courage means being willing to take responsibility for living an aligned life where priorities drive thoughts, feelings and actions to create a sense of deliberateness and purposefulness. Become a man of action and leave your comfort zone, but leave it safely. Don't fall into the trap of feeling guilty for doing what's right for you.

Curiosity

Curiosity fuels discovery, enquiry and learning. It is an ability to relinquish control, be more fluid and question ourselves and our lives to increase the levels of fun, fulfilment and engagement in our everyday experience.

Men who lack high levels of self-esteem will often try to control all aspects of their life; in other words, they can be rigid and resistant to change. I'm calling for men to develop and live life with active curiosity instead of absolute certainty.

Challenge

This value is about embracing challenges, chosen or otherwise, with an enthusiasm that calls you forward to learn, become better and grow from the experience. Don't wait for the right time or motivation: do as the Nike brand instructs, and 'Just do it'. As we saw earlier in the chapter, there is no someday or perfect timing or ideal moment; there is only now.

Connection

Connection to ourselves and others gives meaning and purpose to our lives. At the core of connection is giving ourselves permission to slow down and stop chasing; to be present with ourselves and those we value.

Internally, we create connection when we live in alignment. External connection occurs between people when they feel seen, heard or accepted. I am inviting you as a man to invest your time, effort and energy in creating great connection in your life.

Contribution

The richness of our life is always in direct correlation to our levels of contribution. Musician Bob Marley put it best: 'The greatness of a man is not in how much wealth he acquires, but in his integrity and his ability to affect those around him positively.'

Contribution is about cultivating a deep sense of belonging by connecting and adding our unique skills and experience to the communities we value. If you lead yourself and your communities well, you'll live a 'rich' life.

Consistency

A lack of consistency is tiring, and it can create a sense of both frustration and stagnation for a man. Consistency, therefore, is about developing a deliberate approach to life that compounds our efforts over time, enabling progression and success in all areas.

Because consistency can feel slow, perhaps boring, it's often overlooked, but remember this: sustainable consistency is the fastest way to living a life of success and building a life of significance.

Consider the BetterMen values. They have helped countless men to shift their view on success and recalibrate their lives to live a newly connected, charged and energised experience. Next, we'll dive into how to take these values and translate them into action.

REFLECT, PROJECT, PLAN, DO, REVIEW (RPPDR)

This is a simple strategy I like to employ – it's the one I used to write this book. Succinctly, it means looking back both objectively and subjectively to use our own lived experiences to plan and achieve whatever we want in our future.

Let's elaborate.

Reflect

Self-reflection is the key to self-awareness. Simply put, it's about taking the time to evaluate and give serious thought to our attitudes, feelings and behaviours. It allows us to analyse our lives from both a macro and micro level.

At the macro level, we can assess the overall trajectory of our lives. We can almost do a pre-mortem on where we're heading and determine in advance whether we're happy with our direction. At a micro level, we can evaluate specific responses to circumstances and events.

Both are equally useful, so take a break from your arena of life to reflect. It's well worth it, believe me. Reflection enables you to understand where you've been and what you've experienced so you can really live.

Project

Projecting means looking forward, considering your future, specifically what you want from it and how you want it to feel. It means deciding in advance what you want to experience and intentionally designing your future.

The first step to achieving this is to let your mind wander. Listen to what you intuitively feel you want in your future – not in a default future, but a carefully considered, intentionally designed one.

Let's say, for example, that you want to spend more time with your family. Before you think about the changes you'll need to make, the challenges you're likely to face or how difficult this may be, just let yourself imagine what that life would be like. The moments of deep connection; the making of memories; the shared experiences. Then reverse engineer like so: to get to a future where you'll be spending more time with your loved ones, you'll need to spend less time working. Before doing that, you'll need to understand your financial state and see if that is feasible. Perhaps before understanding your finances, you'll have to talk with financial advisors. You'll also need to start saying no to anything that detracts from your goals at work.

You can use this reverse engineering method to build up a picture of what you want your life to look and feel like so you can start planning to achieve it.

Plan

After you've reflected and projected, create a well thought-out, realistic plan. Canadian psychologist Jordan Peterson said, 'You must specifically determine where in life you're going because you cannot get there unless you consciously move in that direction.' This is exactly right: you need a plan that will create what you have projected. Then you need a plan B in case the first plan doesn't work out.

Do

Now it comes to living above the line of self-leadership and doing the doing. How do you get started with doing? I'd simply encourage you to do more of what works and less of what doesn't. Don't get bored of the basics and adopt an attitude of consistency.

When you're consistent, you'll build up a wave of momentum in your intended direction: don't sabotage yourself, you'll keep going. It's as simple as that.

Review

Once you're on your way, and all the way along your way, objectively review your performance. The most effective way to review performance of any kind is with questions. If you want to know anything, you need to ask questions, and reviewing your own performance is no different.

Continue reviewing your performance with intention until you create your projection and execute your plan.

When you align the four pillars of progression with RPPDR, there's nothing you can't achieve. I have a fantastic reviewing tool that I use with my clients and I'd be happy to share it with you. If you would like to receive it, email me at dan@better-men.uk with the subject line 'Review Tool'.

LIVING, LEADING, LEGACY BUILDING

Men of today, we're pioneers. No other men have lived our digitally connected lives while simultaneously following the old blueprint in the way we have been conditioned to.

We now see that we're at the tipping point and have a responsibility not to pass the same dysfunctional lessons we inherited down to the next generations of men.

No more living life by someone else's expectations, firefighting through your days in a constant state of work-life conflict. It's just not meaningful. Ask yourself what kind of life you want. Once you've decided, say no to everything that isn't exactly aligned to that. Be non-negotiable about who you are and who you are becoming – because the truth is, you're already becoming better.

It's time to stop chasing societal success and instead live a life you're proud of. When you implement it correctly, everything in this chapter will enable you to live and lead a better life and legacy build for tomorrow's men.

Living

What do I mean by living? Longevity isn't a success marker. Just because you experience something – a career, a marriage, a life – for a long time doesn't by default mean it was successful. You get out of life what you put in.

Leading

The best way to create change in life is to lead and role model it. Leading yourself and your family via the BetterMen values and blueprint means keeping your word, taking responsibility and sharing how you feel in every aspect of your life. It means being a leader who people want to follow not just professionally, but also personally. By living life this way, you will get everybody pulling in the same direction, including your family.

Legacy

There comes a point in a man's life where he questions his legacy. He'll hear himself ask questions like, 'Do I matter?' and 'What will I be remembered for?'

A man's legacy is what he passes down to the next generation. The old blueprint forced us to focus primarily on leaving a financial legacy to our children, another mistake. When we're gone, our children won't care about what we bought them; instead, they'll care about how much we loved them and the memories we made with them.

To live a life that outlives you, craft your legacy around what you want to pass on to the next generation. You're learning to rethink masculinity so you can pass on something fit for purpose. If doing so requires change, don't be fearful of implementing it, even if it's starting aspects of your current life again. You won't be starting from scratch; this time, you'll be starting from experience.

Let's get going. Don't tell people what you're going to do, show them. Don't explain your strategy for life, embody it. If you feel like you're in or heading towards a midlife crisis, know you can use it like I did: as midlife re-awakening.

REFLECTION EXERCISES

- If you gave yourself permission to be more expressive, consider at least one thing you'd want to express to each of these groups: family, friends, work colleagues.

- With prevention being better than cure, in which areas of your life do you now recognise you need to be more proactive in? What actions are you aware you need to take?

- Consider the BetterMen values. Which three of the six values, if you deliberately lived from them, would most improve your overall quality of life the most?

- What new thoughts or ideas has reading this book created?

- What have you learned about yourself through reading this book?

- At the end of the first chapter, I asked you to write down the three words that would describe your current life. Remind yourself of these now. Now that you've rethought masculinity and the importance of self-leadership, I am inviting you to look ahead. In a year from now, what three words do you want to describe your life? Compare the two side by side. Do you want your old life or a BetterMen life?

CONCLUSION

You've been on a journey with this book. Now, as you turn the final pages, you continue on as a leader of yourself and a legacy builder in your own life. Know that by implementing even some aspects of what I have shared with you, you are helping to craft something greater than yourself – a new blueprint of masculinity for the generations of men to come after you.

When you work on yourself, everyone benefits. You, me and countless other men are working on themselves: rethinking, reforming and restructuring the concepts of success and masculinity. We're breaking free from the old blueprint and the suffocating myth of masculinity that demands a life of sacrifice and struggle with little fulfilment and reward. We're creating something more intentional, authentic and human that will serve generations to come. What we're passing on matters.

This book, my message, might not be what you thought you needed. If I'd asked men what they wanted, they would have said more... more of everything. That's the exact problem you and I now need to push against – it's a problem we've inherited through parental conditioning, societal expectations and our culture of consumerism. What I have shown you in this book is not how to get more. It's how to get less, but have more.

The great illusion of life is that one day you'll be free of all your problems. That they will dissipate or disappear when you arrive at destination 'success'. The truth is, they won't. Life is a series of problems. The solution to one problem is merely the creation of the next.

Don't search for a life of no problems. Instead, create a life where you get to choose your problems. In his book, *Happy Sexy Millionaire*, *Dragon's Den* investor Steven Bartlett said, 'Sometimes you need to call off the search to find everything you've been looking for.'[1] This is you, calling off your search for more and finding something significantly better than status and success.

Having read this book, you already know all you need to know. If you choose to stay caged or in false comfort, know it's your fears preventing you from turning your new insights into new actions. Remember – everything you want is on the other side of fear.

To live a life you enjoy, a life you're proud of, you need to live in alignment, above the line of self-leadership and employ the four pillars of progression. Life is a process, not an outcome. Stop waiting for the meaning of life to drop into your lap. It's already here.

Enjoy your time and not just in short, fleeting spikes. Doing so comes down to a simple choice, delivered to us in the powerful words of 'Andy', played in the film *The Shawshank Redemption* by actor Tim Robbins. Set against the backdrop of the prison yard, he says, 'Get busy living, or get busy dying.' This is the same choice you, I and every other man has to make. Now you've read my book, my sincere hope is that you will consciously choose to 'get busy living'.

I would like to leave you with a list of key takeaways from each chapter. You can use this as a quick reminder of all you've learned:

- **Chapter 1 key takeaway:** far from serving us, the old and outdated blueprint of masculinity is leading us into workaholism and burnout, loneliness, poor mental health, midlife crises and divorce. There is a better way: the BetterMen blueprint.

- **Chapter 2 key takeaway:** our individual and collective trajectory can be tweaked to empower us to reconnect with our feelings and intuition. We're only ever one thought away from a completely different experience of life.

- **Chapter 3 key takeaway:** it is our time to own where we're at, muster the courage to disrupt what it means to experience the world as a man and make the changes we want to see in the world.

- **Chapter 4 key takeaway:** there are three psychological states to a man's journey: *asleep, aware* and *awake*. Awake is where you want to be; it offers possibilities you don't yet know exist.

- **Chapter 5 key takeaway:** you're at a crossroads in your life. I urge you to choose to leave the old blueprint of masculinity behind and build a strong relationship with yourself.

- **Chapter 6 key takeaway:** to recalibrate your life, you must dismantle the condition you've experienced and learn to trust yourself. With trust, you'll create the capacity to live a life you enjoy.

- **Chapter 7 key takeaway:** to cultivate self-leadership, we cannot be afraid of being assertive and taking the steps necessary to make life happen. First and foremost, become a leader of yourself.

- **Chapter 8 key takeaway:** the only things we leave this world with are our memories and regrets. Make sure that your memories outweigh your regrets. The proper function of a man is to live.

- **Chapter 9 key takeaway:** your time on Earth is finite, so don't waste any more of it before rethinking masculinity and implementing the BetterMen blueprint in your life.

There is no 'someday'. You are ready, own where you are at, and know now is the best time to get started.

Yours in becoming better,

Dan

NEXT STEPS

If you're ready to continue your journey beyond the book, I have created a free resource library which you can find on my website (www.better-men.uk).

This contains, among other things, interactive scorecards for benchmarking both your work-life integration and susceptibility to a midlife crisis, press articles and actionable blogs, and my acclaimed monthly newsletter, *The BetterMen Bulletin*.

Additionally, under the resources section of my website, you'll find my podcast appearances in which you can hear me discuss a range of topics relating to modern masculinity, leadership and self-development.

Beyond this, if you're interested in personalised support, I'd encourage you to consider my coaching services. I offer a range of proven options, each of which supports men to live better lives through a systemised combination of High-Performance Coaching™, Neuro-Linguistic Programming (NLP) and Behavioural Change Technologies.

Recommended specifically for readers of this book is my Better Yourself course. It carries the same themes and development opportunities as *Rethinking Masculinity*. With the Better Yourself course, you'll join and collaborate with other like-minded men for nine weeks. Collectively, you will be equipped with the tools to get clarity in your life, motivate you to live more productively and establish a sense of purpose to accomplish your life goals.

Speaking

Dan is an experienced, charismatic speaker who continuously engages and inspires his audience. He is an expert at speaking on a range of topics, from modern-day masculinity to men's performance and wellbeing. He is equally adept at facilitating digital or physical speaking engagements, including keynote speaking, conferences and podcast appearances. To enquire about speaking engagements, email dan@better-men.uk.

REFERENCES

Introduction

1   Alighieri, D, *Inferno* (Alma Classics, 2014) translated by JG Nichols

Chapter 1: Twenty-first Century Masculinity

1   Dr Derler, A, 'Burnt out Britain' (*Visier*) www.visier.com/blog/trends/burnt-out-britain, accessed 26 January 2022

2   'Stages of burnout' (Stress – Burnout Stages) www.winona.edu/stress/bntstages.htm, accessed 26 January 2022

3   Ibbetson, C, 'How many people don't have a best friend?' (*YouGov*) https://yougov.co.uk/topics/relationships/articles-reports/2019/09/25/quarter-britons-dont-have-best-friend, accessed 26 January 2022

4   'Millions of men are hiding their loneliness' (Campaign to End Loneliness, 2017) www.campaigntoendloneliness.org/millions-of-men-are-hiding-their-loneliness, accessed 26 January 2022

5   Ipsos Public Affairs, 'Perceptions of masculinity and the challenges of opening up' (November, 2019) https://cdn.movember.com/uploads/images/2012/News/UK%20IRE%20ZA/Movember%20Masculinity%20%26%20Opening%20Up%20Report%2008.10.19%20FINAL.pdf, accessed 27 January 2022

6   Ipsos Public Affairs, 'Perceptions of masculinity and the challenges of opening up' (November, 2019) https://cdn.movember.com/uploads/images/2012/News/UK%20IRE%20ZA/Movember%20Masculinity%20%26%20Opening%20Up%20Report%2008.10.19%20FINAL.pdf, accessed 27 January 2022

7   Ipsos Public Affairs, 'Perceptions of masculinity and the challenges of opening up' (November, 2019) https://cdn.movember.com/uploads/images/2012/News/UK%20IRE%20ZA/Movember%20Masculinity%20%26%20Opening%20Up%20Report%2008.10.19%20FINAL.pdf, accessed 27 January 2022

8   Pandya, A; Lodha, P, 'Social connectedness, excessive screen time during COVID-19 and mental health: A review of current evidence' (Frontiers in Human Dynamics, 2021) www.frontiersin.org/articles/10.3389/fhumd.2021.684137/full, accessed 27 June 2022

9   'The health benefits of strong relationships' (*Harvard Health Publishing*, 2010) www.health.harvard.edu/staying-healthy/the-health-benefits-of-strong-relationships, accessed 26 January 2022

10   'Men' (BeyondBlue) www.beyondblue.org.au/who-does-it-affect/men, accessed 27 January 2022

11   Nasir, R; John, E; Windsor-Shellard, B, 'Suicides in England and Wales: 2020 registrations' (Office for National Statistics) www.ons.gov.uk/peoplepopulationandcommunity/birthsdeathsandmarriages/deaths/bulletins/suicidesintheunitedkingdom/2020registrations, accessed 27 January 2022

12   'Men and mental health' (Mental Health Foundation, 2021) www.mentalhealth.org.uk/a-to-z/m/men-and-mental-health, accessed 27 Jan 2022

13   Divorce statistics (Crisp&Co, 2022) www.crispandco.com/site/divorce-statistics, accessed 27 January 2022

14   'Why have divorce rates increased during the Covid-19 pandemic?' (Stewarts, 2021) www.stewartslaw.com/news/why-have-divorce-rates-increased-during-the-covid-19-pandemic, accessed 28 January 2022

15   Robbins, A, *Awaken the Giant Within: How to take immediate control of your mental, emotional, physical and financial destiny* (Simon & Schuster, 2001)

Chapter 2: The History of Modern-day Masculinity

1   'Industrialization, Labor, and Life' (*National Geographic*) www.nationalgeographic.org/article/industrialization-labor-and-life/7th-grade, accessed 2 February 2022

2   'Killed, wounded and missing' (*Britannica*) www.britannica.com/event/World-War-I/Killed-wounded-and-missing, accessed 2 February 2022

3   'Research starters: Worldwide deaths in World War II' (The National WWII Museum) www.nationalww2museum.org/students-teachers/student-resources/research-starters/research-starters-worldwide-deaths-world-war, accessed 2 February 2022

4   Turnbull, GJ, 'A review of post-traumatic stress disorder. Part I: Historical development and classification' (National Library of Medicine, March 1998) 29(2):87–91 https://pubmed.ncbi.nlm.nih.gov/10721399, accessed 27 June 2022

5   O'Connor, M, 'The shocking cost of fatherlessness in the UK' (The London Economic) www.thelondoneconomic.com/opinion/the-shocking-cost-of-fatherlessness-in-the-uk-33143, accessed 6 February 2022

6   'Where have all the men gone?' (FullFact, 12 June 2013) https://fullfact.org/news/where-have-all-men-gone, accessed 8 February 2022

7   'Statistics on fatherlessness in America and the profound impact of mentoring' (No Longer Fatherless) www.nolongerfatherless.org/statistics, accessed 10 February 2022

8   Bronte-Tinkew, J, Moore, C & Zaff, J, 'The influence of father involvement on youth risk behaviors among adolescents: A comparison of native-born and immigrant families', Social Science Research (2006) https://doi.org/10.1016/j.ssresearch.2004.08.002, accessed 27 June 2022

9   O'Connor, B, 'Rise of the female breadwinner: Woman earns the most in one-in-four households' (Royal London, 27 May 2020) www.royallondon.com/media/press-releases/archive/female-breadwinner-rise, accessed 15 February 2022

10   Partridge, J, 'Number of FTSE 100 female directors rises by 50% in five years' (*The Guardian*, 23 February 2021) www.theguardian.com/business/2021/feb/23/number-of-ftse-100-women-directors-rises-by-50-in-five-years, accessed 15 February 2022

11   Early, B, (Oprah Daily, 10 Feb 2022) The Five Love Languages, Explained www.oprahdaily.com/life/relationships-love/a28084004/five-love-languages-summary, accessed 27 June 2022

Chapter 3: Middle-aged Masculinity

1   Gayle, D, 'People aged 40–59 are least happy and most anxious, report finds' (*The Guardian*, 2 February 2016) www.theguardian.com/society/2016/feb/02/middle-aged-people-least-happy-most-anxious-ons-wellbeing-report, accessed 25 February 2022

2   Steiner, S, 'Top regrets of the dying' (*The Guardian*, 1 February 2012) www.theguardian.com/lifeandstyle/2012/feb/01/top-five-regrets-of-the-dying, accessed 28 February 2022

3   'Daily time spent on social networking by internet users worldwide from 2012 to 2022' (Statista, 21 March 2022) www.statista.com/statistics/433871/daily-social-media-usage-worldwide, accessed 22 March 2022

4   Silva, C, 'Social media's impact on self-esteem' (*Huffington Post*, 22 February 2017) www.huffpost.com/entry/social-medias-impact-on-self-esteem_b_58ade038e4b0d818c4f0a4e4, accessed 22 March 2022

5   Caceres, V, 'Happiness is about 40% genetic, but you can control it – here are 8 ways to feel happier every day' (*Business Insider*, 18 May 2022) www.insider.com/is-happiness-genetic, accessed 27 June 2022

6   Mahdawi, A, 'Can cities kick ads? Inside the global movement to ban urban billboards' (*The Guardian*, 12 August 2015) www.theguardian.com/cities/2015/aug/11/can-cities-kick-ads-ban-urban-billboards, accessed 25 March 2022

7   Brittle, Z, 'When three's not the charm: How to manage the higher risk of divorce when baby comes along' (*The Washington Post*, 30 June 2015) www.washingtonpost.com/news/inspired-life/wp/2015/06/30/when-threes-not-the-charm-how-to-manage-the-higher-risk-of-divorce-when-baby-comes-along, accessed 25 March 2022

8   Cohn, D'V, 'About a fifth of US adults moved due to COVID-19 or know someone who did' (Pew Research, 6 July 2020) www.pewresearch.org/fact-tank/2020/07/06/about-a-fifth-of-u-s-adults-moved-due-to-covid-19-or-know-someone-who-did, accessed 25 March 2022

9   US Census Bureau and the US Department of Housing and Urban Development, Monthly New Residential Sales (26 April 2022) www.census.gov/construction/nrs/pdf/newressales.pdf, accessed 20 June 2022

10   Rashida, K, 'Quitting is just half the story: the truth behind the Great Resignation' (The Guardian, 4 January 2022) www.theguardian.com/business/2022/jan/04/great-resignation-quitting-us-unemployment-economy

11   Men's mental health trends July and August 2020, On the Line, (2016) https://ontheline.org.au/mental-health-blog/mens-mental-health-statistics, accessed 27 June 2022

Chapter 4: No Man's Land

1   'Why 85% of people hate their jobs' (Staff Squared, 3 December 2019) https://staffsquared.com/blog/why-85-of-people-hate-their-jobs, accessed 27 March 2022

2   Donovan, F, 'Shocking stats show guys are still under extreme pressure to "Man Up"' (Unilad, 22 June 2017) www.unilad.co.uk/featured/shocking-stats-show-guys-are-still-under-pressure-to-man-up, accessed 27 March 2022

3   Scutti, S, Michael Phelps: 'I am extremely thankful that I did not take my life', CNN (2018) https://edition.cnn.com/2018/01/19/health/michael-phelps-depression/index.html, accessed 27 June 2022

4   'I walked off after the 2003 World Cup hating rugby says Jonny Wilkinson' (The Rugby Paper, April 2019) www.therugbypaper.co.uk/latest-news/32556/i-hated-rugby-after-2003-rugby-world-cup-says-jonny-wilkinson/, accessed 27 June 2022

5   Hill, C, 'Retirement is making people more miserable than ever before' (MarketWatch, 2 July 2016) www.marketwatch.com/story/retirement-is-making-people-more-miserable-than-ever-before-2016-06-30, accessed 30 March 2022

6   'Why do retirees die soon after retirement?' (Elder Guru) www.elderguru.com/why-do-retirees-die-soon-after-retirement, accessed 1 April 2022

7   Joint news release: 'Long working hours increasing deaths from heart disease and stroke: WHO, ILO' (World Health Organization, 17 May 2021) www.who.int/news/item/17-05-2021-long-working-hours-increasing-deaths-from-heart-disease-and-stroke-who-ilo, accessed 1 April 2022

8   'National life tables – life expectancy in the UK: 2018 to 2020' (ONS, 23 September 2021) www.ons.gov.uk/peoplepopulationandcommunity/birthsdeathsandmarriages/lifeexpectancies/bulletins/nationallifetablesunitedkingdom/2018to2020, accessed 1 April 2022

9   Orwell, G, 'Shooting an elephant' (Burmese Days, The Orwell Foundation) www.orwellfoundation.com/the-orwell-foundation/orwell/essays-and-other-works/shooting-an-elephant, accessed 27 June 2022

10   Kounang, N, 'What is the science behind fear?' (CNN, 29 October 2015) https://edition.cnn.com/2015/10/29/health/science-of-fear/index.html, accessed 4 April 2022

11   'How many thoughts do we have per minute?' (Reference, 8 April 2020) www.reference.com/world-view/many-thoughts-per-minute-cb7fcf22ebbf8466, accessed 4 April 2022

Chapter 5: The Choice

1   Brooks, D, *The Second Mountain: A stirring guide to escaping the prison of self* (Penguin, 2020)

2   Rhor, R, *Adam's Return: The Five Promises of Male Initiation* (Independent Publishers Group, 2004)

3   Jeffery, S, 'How to Use the Hero's Journey for Personal Development' (CEOSAGE) https://scottjeffrey.com/heros-journey-steps, accessed 20 June 2022

4   Groysberg, B & Abrahams, R, 'What the Stockdale Paradox Tells Us About Crisis Leadership' (Harvard Business School, August 2020) https://hbswk. hbs.edu/item/what-the-stockdale-paradox-tells-us-about-crisis-leadership, accessed 20 June 2022

5   Brown, B, Podcast, Unlocking Us: Anxiety, Calm, and Over-/Under-Functioning www.brenebrown.com/podcast/brene-on-anxiety-calm-over-under-functioning/, accessed 20 Jun 2022

6   Kaufman, SB, 'Unraveling the mindset of victimhood' (*Scientific American*, 2020) www.scientificamerican.com/article/unraveling-the-mindset-of-victimhood, accessed 27 June 2022

7   Singer, M, *Untethered Soul: The journey beyond yourself* (New Harbinger, 2007)

Chapter 6: Recalibrating Our Lives

1   Canfield, J, 'The success formula that puts you in control of your destiny' (Jack Canfield Maximizing Your Potential, blog post) https://jackcanfield. com/blog/the-formula-that-puts-you-in-control-of-success, accessed 27 June 2022

2   Cherry, K, 'What is the negativity bias?' (Very Well Mind, 29 April 2020) www.verywellmind.com/negative-bias-4589618, accessed 20 April 2022

3   'Two Wolves: A Cherokee legend' (First People) www.firstpeople.us/FP-Html-Legends/TwoWolves-Cherokee.html, accessed 21 April 2022

4   'How many thoughts do we have per minute?' (Reference, 8 April 2020) www.reference.com/world-view/many-thoughts-per-minute-cb7fcf22ebbf8466, accessed 4 April 2022

5   Peterson, A, 'What Is... the Frequency Illusion (Baader-Meinhof Phenomenon)' (Mental Health @ Home, December 2021) www.mentalhealthathome.org/2021/12/03/what-is-frequency-illusion/, accessed 21 June 2022

6   Anwar, Y, 'How many different human emotions are there?' (*Greater Good Magazine*, 8 September 2017) https://greatergood.berkeley.edu/article/item/how_many_different_human_emotions_are_there, accessed 27 April 2022

7   American Friends of Tel Aviv University, 'Going with your gut feeling: Intuition alone can guide right choice, study suggests' (Science Daily, 8 November 2012) www.sciencedaily.com/releases/2012/11/121108131724.htm, accessed 1 May 2022

Chapter 7: Self-leadership

1   Wilson, J, (@mrjasonowilson) 'A man who has to walk on eggshells to keep peace, will become so skilled at it that he makes no sound in life.' (Tweet, 24 March 2022) https://twitter.com/mrjasonowilson/status/1506971248248635401?lang=bg, accessed 27 June 2022

2   Goleman, D, *Emotional Intelligence: Why it can matter more than IQ* (Bantam, 2005)

3   Voss, P, 'Dynamic brains and the changing rules of neuroplasticity: Implications for learning and recovery' (Frontiers in Psychology, 2017) www.frontiersin.org/article/10.3389/fpsyg.2017.01657, accessed 27 June 2022

4   Society for Personality and Social Psychology, 'How we form habits, change existing ones' (ScienceDaily, August 2014) www.sciencedaily.com/releases/2014/08/140808111931.htm, accessed 27 June 2022

5   Parker Fischer, C; Romero, LM, 'Chronic captivity stress in wild animals is highly species-specific' (*Conservation Physiology*, 7.1, 2019) www.ncbi.nlm.nih.gov/pmc/articles/PMC6892464, accessed 27 June 2022

6   Dispenza, J, 'Aligning Your Environments To Tomorrow's You', Unlimited (2016) https://drjoedispenza.com/blogs/dr-joes-blog/part-ii-aligning-your-environments-to-tomorrow-s-you, accessed 27 June 2022

7   Stone, AM, '90 seconds to emotional resilience' (Alyson M Stone, 19 November 2018) www.alysonmstone.com/90-seconds-to-emotional-resilience, accessed 5 May 2022

8   Advaney, M, 'To talk or not to talk that is the question!' (*Youth Time Magazine*, 5 June 2017) https://youth-time.eu/to-talk-or-not-to-talk-that-is-the-question-at-least-70-percent-of-communication-is-non-verbal, accessed 20 April 2022

9   Fiorenzi, R, 'How your chair may be hurting you' (Start Standing, 5 March 2022) www.startstanding.org/sitting-new-smoking/#para18, accessed 20 March 2022

10   MacVean, M, '"Get Up!" or lose hours of your life every day, scientist says (*Los Angeles Times*, 31 July 2014) www.latimes.com/science/sciencenow/la-sci-sn-get-up-20140731-story.html, accessed 27 June 2022

11   Raphael, R, 'Netflix CEO Reed Hastings: Sleep Is Our Competition' (Fast Company, 6 November 2017) www.fastcompany.com/40491939/netflix-ceo-reed-hastings-sleep-is-our-competition, assessed 20 June 2022

12   Rogers, A, *I'm Only Human After All*, The Empowerment Series Book 1 (CreateSpace Independent Publishing Platform, 2011)

13   Lapp, L., and Davidson, L., 'Resilience: The Ways To Enhance This Critical Skill In Sports', Broadview Psychology (2020) http://broadviewpsychology.com/2020/04/21/resilience-the-ways-to-enhance-this-critical-skill-in-sports/, accessed 27 June 2022

14   Robbins, A, *Awaken the Giant Within: How to take immediate control of your mental, emotional, physical and financial destiny* (Simon & Schuster, 2001)

Chapter 8: Life Isn't A Rehearsal

1   Dalio, R, *Principles* (Simon & Schuster, 2017)

2   Collins, J, *Good To Great: Why some companies make the leap... and others don't* (Random House, 2001)

3   Darwin Correspondence Project (Cambridge University Library) 'The evolution of a misquotation', www.darwinproject.ac.uk/people/about-darwin/six-things-darwin-never-said/evolution-misquotation, accessed 21 June 2022

4   Renner, B, 'Survey: Average adult rates their happiness level at just 6.3 out of 10' (Study Finds, 23 September 2019), www.studyfinds.org/survey-average-adult-rates-their-happiness-level-at-just-6-3-out-of-10, accessed 20 March 2022

5   Wagner, A, 'A decade of data reveals that heavy multitaskers have reduced memory, Stanford psychologist says', Stanford News (25 October 2018), https://news.stanford.edu/2018/10/25/decade-data-reveals-heavy-multitaskers-reduced-memory-psychologist-says/, accessed 27 June 2022

6   Allen, D, *Getting Things Done: The Art of Stress-Free Productivity* (Piatkus, March 2015)

7   Wen, T, BBC: Worklife, 'The 'law' that explains why you can't get anything done' (22 May 2020) www.bbc.com/worklife/article/20191107-the-law-that-explains-why-you-cant-get-anything-done, accessed 21 June 2022

8   Suni, E, 'How much sleep do we really need?' (Sleep Foundation, 13 April 2022) www.sleepfoundation.org/how-sleep-works/how-much-sleep-do-we-really-need, accessed 20 April 2022

9   Shannon, J, *Don't Feed The Monkey Mind: How to stop the cycle of anxiety, fear, and worry* (New Harbinger, 2017)

Chapter 9: Becoming Better

1   Willcox, G, 'The Feeling Wheel: A tool for expanding awareness of emotions and increasing spontaneity and intimacy, (*Transactional Analysis Journal*, 1982) www.tandfonline.com/doi/abs/10.1177/036215378201200411, accessed 27 June 2022

Conclusion

1   Bartlett, S, *Happy Sexy Millionaire: Unexpected truths about Fulfilment, Love and Success* (Yellow Kite, 2021)

ACKNOWLEDGEMENTS

Writing a book about masculinity, personal development and self-leadership never felt like it would be an easy endeavour, but I didn't expect that the journey would feel like one of the most important things I have done with my life. In the first half of my life, anything of significance I achieved, I did so seeking the validation of others. Now in the second half of my life, not needing validation any longer, I mustered my own motivation and leveraged the BetterMen methodologies to produce a book I'm proud of.

This book wouldn't have been possible without the broad network of thought leaders I have worked with since founding BetterMen. Those I have coached, those I have connected with and those I have learned from. Firstly, I'd like to thank Daniel Priestley for planting the seed about writing a book. Thank you also to Lucy Cohen for reinforcing this by stating I should write a book over a bottle of wine, and to Gaby Brogan for superbly guiding me through the process.

A special thanks to Phil Davies for writing the foreword to this book and for being a man among men. To Joe Gregory and the team at Rethink Press for efficiently polishing my manuscript and taking personal interest in my project. Thanks also to my beta readers: Dave Dayman, Jackie Royall, Mark Hindmarsh, Martin Thompson, Marilise de Villiers, Michael Griffiths, Neal Reed, Nick Davies, Ollie Rastall, Phil Glover, Ricki Takooree for providing their honest commentary on my manuscript draft and to Bradley Lever of The Content Creators for my headshot.

Thank you to Andy Kershaw and Lyle McRae for being my brothers and, of course, to all of my past clients: the men who have placed their trust in me. To all of my future clients – know that the journey is always worth it.

THE AUTHOR

Dan Stanley is a retired award-winning senior Army commando, a key decision maker in a multi-million-pound service business and a former national sporting champion in indoor rowing. He is also an expert in men's development and performance.

After the birth of his first child, Dan experienced a midlife crisis. His life situation forced him to accept his failings as a man and become a better version of himself. He embarked on a journey of introspection, personal growth and deliberate action to become an emotionally aware yet resilient and assertive man. His journey was turbulent but transformative; he turned his midlife crisis into a midlife transformation.

Years later, leveraging his own experience, Dan founded BetterMen, a coaching practice working exclusively with men. In this role, he has coached hundreds of clients, helping them improve their wellbeing, relationships and lives. His work has empowered clients to change or re-ignite their careers, save their marriages, exit businesses for seven-figure sums and gain investment in the BBC's Dragon's Den.

Additionally, Dan is the facilitator of Men & Mountains, a men's walking community with hundreds of members across the UK. He works as a wellbeing ambassador for Project RECCE, a charity that supports the successful transition of military veterans into sustained employment within the construction industry. Dan contributes frequently to national publications such as *Men's Fitness* and *Muscle and Health* magazine.

You can connect with Dan via:

 www.better-men.uk

 Dan@better-men.uk

 www.linkedin.com/in/dan-stanley-bettermen

Printed in Great Britain
by Amazon

18869541R00113